D1743801

I

CAME HERE

TO

TAKE YOUR JOB

By

Eva S.

Grosvenor House
Publishing Limited

This book is published by
Grosvenor House Publishing Ltd
Link House
140 The Broadway, Tolworth, Surrey, Kt6 7Ht.
www.grosvenorhousepublishing.co.uk

A CIP record for this book
is available from the British Library

ISBN 978-1-83975-224-7

Dedication

For everybody that recognises themselves in the story, either
directly or indirectly - this story is for you.

But most of all, it is for my mom, grandma,
and three sisters - it's about time you found out
what really happened.

Contents

~

1

Look at me. Don't you just hate me already? I don't speak like you, I come from a country you've probably never heard of, and you can see from miles away that I have zero English blood in me. According to some of the British media, I was born to take your job. *I am* the reason for everything bad happening in your country. Well, here I am, nice to meet you! I am Eva.

I can't remember much of my childhood, nor do I think you'd really care. But in order to really understand why I left my life behind and jumped into the unknown, one must start from the very beginning. As therapists always say when you wind up at their office, lost, confused, and most definitely about to cry, 'Tell me about your childhood.' So… here I go.

I grew up in Estonia in the 1990s. Technically, I was still born in the Soviet Union, because Estonia regained its independence only seven months after my birth. Of course, the Soviet Union was already thoroughly broken by the time I was brought into this world. And, despite the freedom, the 90s was still a tough decade for our little country.

It was August 1991 when Estonia became free again. We first got our independence in 1918, but that only lasted until 1940 when we were forced back under the Russian law. Before that, we had also been under German law, Swedish law, Danish law, and God knows who else's. Nowadays, whenever anybody asks why Estonian women are so good-looking, the answer is that we've been screwed over by so many different countries that… well, something good had to come out of it, at least.

By 1991, the USSR was destroyed and all the countries in eastern Europe started to declare their independence one after another. They were like the first seeds that grow on an empty, harsh soil without really knowing what they're supposed to do. It wasn't easy – 51 years of occupation is a long time. It can break even the toughest man. Most of the people had never lived in a free country before. My own grandmother, who was then in her forties, had never lived in an independent Estonia, nor my mother. Nobody knew how to fly with the wings that they had never used.

For over four decades, we hadn't been free. Closed from the world, deprived of free speech and real opportunities, all eastern European countries had been waiting for their turn to get out of Soviet rule and become independent once more. But when it finally happened, life wasn't easy at all.

In the 90s, Estonia was probably best known for its high crime, poor economy, alcoholism, and high death rates… that's if it was known at all. Inflation and unemployment were at its highest; all the old ways had been destroyed, yet a stable, strong foundation from which to build your future, didn't yet exist. The only thing that kept people going was the hope of a better future and the fact that at least now, we were free. Even though it tasted bittersweet.

I was a child and didn't really care nor understand what was happening around me. Only years later did I realise the reasons behind some of the inexplicable aspects of daily life that I had come to see as normal.

Estonia was a mess. People didn't know how to be, what to do. It was completely normal to see drunk people at my great-grandma's early in the afternoon, crying over a bottle of vodka. Or to see sleeping men in the outside cafe, sometimes covered in their own piss while others around them were having coffee and cake.

One of the favourite places for me and my friends to play at was the back of a motel which had these large, beautiful stairs. We spent most of our free time there. The motel had been abandoned for years by that point, and the stairs were full of tumbleweed, stones, and heaps of bloody syringes. We pretended the motel was our kingdom and cleaned its stairs for our beautiful home, careful not to touch the needles. But it was a never-ending job; if we cleaned them one day, the needles were back a few days later.

But that was all fine. As a child, you don't really judge, I think. You do have a sense of right and wrong and we knew those syringes weren't great, but everybody was welcomed in our little kingdom. All the drunks, all the junkies, all the adults and other children. No judgment there. I never minded my great-grandma's alcohol-fuelled friends, either. They'd always bring me sweets and books, and they hugged me so much I started to think this transparent liquor must be love in a bottle.

My great-grandmother was a big, serious woman with white hair, who never drank and hardly spoke – even to her own friends. All she really cared about was getting food on the table for her family while listening to her neighbours gossip about anybody but her. Needless to say, she was so busy doing this that she didn't have any time to hug me much. I hung out more with her friends than with my great-grandmother herself. To me, stale alcohol smells meant chocolate-covered candies, old books, and lots of hugs from funky-smelling, shivering adults with red, sad faces.

If I wasn't hanging out with my great-grandmother and her friends, I was with my mom and older sister. We lived in a small flat on the highest floor. We were so high up you could see all of our little town from the big windows in our bedroom. It was quite grey, dark, and sad, to be honest – even for a young girl like me. There was nothing but low, dirty buildings, and tired, intoxicated people staggering in its hollow, lifeless streets.

But there was one thing that was the most beautiful sight I thought I had ever seen – a Ferris wheel. When I looked outside my window, I could see it a little further away. Amongst all of this sadness and grey existence, there was this bright yellow beauty, the only colourful thing in town. This was the only indicator that there was still life in this world, riding people into happiness with its every turn.

For my 5-year-old child's brain, this was the most beautiful thing in the world. I thought it was where the rich people went when they grew up. There, you could buy a ticket to eternal happiness. If only my great-grandma's friends knew that a ride on a Ferris wheel was all they needed to feel good, they would never cry nor drink again. I tried to explain this to them, but they only smiled back and had another sip and a cry. Not wanting to turn out like them, I promised myself I would go there first thing when I grew up.

My mom was a single mother who worked a lot to keep us going. She loves music, clothes, and has a funny sense of humour, making her quite charming. Unfortunately, the fact that she had two little kids at such an early age in her life meant that she never got to live out her real self. Instead of having fun like a young woman should, she had to do stressful jobs and deal with two crazy kids. Fortunately for her, my older sister has always been the better one – more obedient and well behaved; the perfect child. Since I was the total opposite, we argued and fought constantly. Because of this, I ended up spending a lot of time with my grandmother and great-grandmother.

I loved staying at my grandmother's. She was just as strong and quiet as her mother, and just as big, but she had fiery red hair and even fiercer personality that radiated through her strong work ethics, direct words, and brown eyes . In the Soviet Union, she had tried to hide her hair by dying it blonde her whole life, for fear of standing out too much. Now, she had had enough of pretending in every way. She was letting her short, red hair run free while embracing everything Western our new little country could offer. When she wanted a doughnut and a coffee, she walked like a trooper through all the syringes and piss lying on the ground without even blinking an eye. All I could do was to keep up with her and her ambition; I admired and was scared of her, at the same time.

Being a new-age, Western grandmother, she had a satellite TV with about 20 channels. It was a real luxury to have a colour TV with foreign channels in the 90s' Estonia. My mom's TV, for example, only had the boring three channels Estonia offered at the time, while I had all the world in front of my eyes at grandmother's.

After spending a day at my great-grandma's, playing in her garden, discovering bugs, nature, and also that too much love in a bottle will kill you sooner or later, I'd go to my grandma's and watch Cartoon Network for hours. She would buy me all the sweets, crisps, and drinks anybody could wish for, without ever thinking about what horrible effect it would have on the health of a child who had already spent the day eating choco-late and breathing in alcohol fumes.

I remember clearly the day it all changed.

After the usual day full of drunken complaints and hugs, followed by sugarshop tour and Cartoon Network, my grand-mother decided she'd had enough of Tom and Jerry sounds. She took the remote control and changed it to a random music channel, angrily taking the remote control with her. Surprised by my grandma's sudden outburst, her (apparent) hate for cartoons, and my own inability to understand what

I was now watching, I was baffled. I didn't say a word. It was as if she had said, without using any words, that I should grow up. And I had no other option but to obey.

I looked at the screen. Music was blasting out. I had never heard anything like that. These were real people. They were saying actual words, none of which I understood. But they were cool, young, and hip. There were all sorts of colours, hairstyles, and clothes. Black, yellow, white people, jumping, singing, dancing on big city streets, moving their bodies in ways I had never seen before. Tall, concrete buildings, lots of traffic, cars beeping, people enjoying themselves. They were loud, confident, and looked like they were having so much fun.

I did not understand what I was watching. Where were the motels with syringes in the front? Where were the drunk, crying people? Why were these people so happy? Nobody was ever that happy; I knew that already.

I watched these music videos for hours, until it came time to go to bed. And even then, I couldn't stop thinking about what I had just seen. I had never encountered anything like that in my life. The only people I had seen had all been white, mostly blonde and blue-eyed, usually hungover from the previous day or still drunk, and definitely sick of life. So, who were these people in this TV?

I became obsessed. I realised at that moment that there was a life more vibrant, bigger, and bolder than the one I was in. And I became determined to be part of it. Right there, right then.

And from that moment on, my life was changed forever. VH1 became my new best friend, and my grandmother learned to work to the sounds of the latest music hits. I didn't understand a single word nor did I care; the images alone fulfilled my every wish. I was like a poor kid that was window shopping for her better life, counting down the time and money till she could have a taste of one.

I never wanted to leave grandma's house again. I wanted to watch TV all the time and look at the world that I was already living in inside my head. I started to crave for things I didn't know the name of and had only seen on foreign channels.

Real life started to feel like a drag and I couldn't talk to my great-grandma's friends any more. "You, girl, are talking about life far, far away, in the fancy land, somewhere that we will never get to, never be part of. Let it go. Stop dancing like this. What are these words you're saying? That ain't Estonian. Girl, you need to come back down to earth, that life ain't for us," they'd tell me when I talked about the magical things I had seen on TV. I'd show them the new dance moves from the foreign videos, bending my limbs and body in ways I had seen the happy people do, but they weren't impressed.

'Your great-granddaughter's gone crazy, look at her. What is she saying, doing? It's weird. A woman needs to know how to cook and when to shut up, and not watch this crazy foreign stuff on the telly. It will bring her no good. No good,' they'd tell my great-grandmother. She'd then try unsuccessfully to tame me, because she was embarrassed in front of her friends. She never wanted to be their reason for gossiping.

It felt like the bottle of love they had been drinking had been switched with a bottle of pure crap, and I didn't want to be part of any of that. They didn't believe the life I knew I was gonna live, and I didn't believe them when they told me people 'like us' could never be that happy and live that life. Who was this 'us'? Who was this 'them'? Aren't we all just people, living, crying, and loving the same way?

I didn't understand them; they didn't understand me. From that moment on, I started to stay away from them, because I knew I was going to go to the streets I'd seen on the telly the moment I could. Also, they began to die, one by one, due to all the transparent love they were constantly sculling down.

To be honest, every moment I spent away from my grand-mother's TV felt like a waste of time. I wasn't dreaming of getting older and bigger and finding out what happiness the Ferris wheel held anymore. Now, I knew I was gonna go away, far further than that Ferris wheel. All I wanted to do was go to a place that had skyscrapers, and traffic, and colourful people all happily dancing on the streets. That's where I was going to go.

And I would have, too, if we hadn't moved and I'd had to start school, which delayed my plans for the next thirteen years. My mother gave birth to my two little sisters some years later. Going to school, making friends, going through life and its changes played with me a lot - - as it does to all of us. But no matter what was happening in my life, I knew where I wanted to end up.

I began collecting money when I was about ten years old so that I would have a head-start to my new life when I was older. Every day, I'd put half of my lunch money in a shoebox, and only opened it when I wanted to buy a foreign magazine or a cassette.

I didn't have any high hopes. Even though I had just started school, I knew I wasn't gonna be great at it, nor did I care. I already knew what my plan was going to be. And whenever anybody told me to stop watching 'that foreign crap and stop dreaming of what will never be', I turned the other way. There was no point in arguing. They would never understand the life much bigger that I was talking about, just like I didn't under-stand the narrow, small-minded world they tried to push me into.

We were two types of people that had come from the same place, looked the same, and did the same things... while living in completely different worlds.

I graduated in 2010. I felt so happy. Relieved. Excited. Liberated. After twelve years of feeling like I had no control over my life, and forced to obey some silly rules that often made no sense to me (nor even to the people who were preaching them), I finally started to see the light at the end of this long, dark tunnel of mine. I had served my duty. I had done my part. Now I was free. And, oh boy, did it feel sweet.

Just as I had changed, so had Estonia. We joined the EU in 2004, opening our borders to the world, cleaned up our streets, and focused on becoming the best IT country out there. But this decision didn't come easily. Becoming part of the EU was regarded as joining another union where we had to follow others' laws. It had been thirteen years since we had managed to get out of one, and nobody had the desire to step into the same hole again. Nevertheless, 66% of people decided to vote for the EU and, with that, we were in.

During the following years, Estonia really struggled due to high emigration. For the first time in forever, people were free to go and live anywhere, travel everywhere, and not have to worry about having visas or being killed on the way. Many went to live and work in Finland, where they could live a similar life while getting better wages, mostly ending up as construction workers or as cleaners.

In the meantime, Estonia was making huge progress in the IT field, becoming a cool little country that had started to make a name for itself for other things besides drinking and crime.

I had survived my time in school thanks to my four amazing friends. Together, we shared the idea of foreign adventures, music, books, and life. Since none of us was interested in anything IT-related , we couldn't wait until graduation so that we could go and explore what the rest of the world had to offer us – just like thousands of other Estonians.

We were completely and utterly obsessed with everything from the other side of the border, whether it was art, fashion, people, or the countries themselves. It was all that we talked about, thought about, and wanted.

My dream had always been to go to France. In my head, I could imagine myself wandering through the streets of Paris like the poets, painters, and artists had done back in the 1920s and 30s. Our other options were to become an au pair, a go-go dancer, or a volunteer abroad, but none of these options sparked my interest as much as my imaginary life in Paris.

I was living in Tallinn a week after the graduation. But as it turned out, I was the only one from my friends who was still holding onto the foreign dream. Everybody else was applying for universities and finding their own place in Estonia, not even wanting to discuss any of our past thoughts or promises.

I felt devastated. For me, there was no other option but leaving Estonia. It had been my dream since I could first remember, and the only light and reason to get me through school in the first place.

Because of the failed dreams, I applied to university as well. I chose to study Roman languages – still holding onto my French dream – but I wasn't even excited when they informed me I had been accepted. My only reason for applying was so that I could take part in the Erasmus study abroad programme the following year, which is offered to the good students.

I started living in a youth hostel right in the heart of Tallinn, but I must admit, I was very hesitant at first. I had no desire to live there, and no desire to attend university. All I wanted was to go to France and never look back.

But as soon as the door opened and I saw a skinny, sleepy-eyed, gel-haired, over-perfumed boy welcoming me in, I knew I was going to live in this hostel… and I was in big trouble. At that moment, France had nothing on that boy. I was so smitten by him I couldn't even focus on what the house actually looked like nor what was said.

Me and my room-mate were the one of the only Estonian girls in the house: there were people from Czech Republic, Hungary, Australia, England, France, Finland, Georgia, plus all the artists that came into our house every now and again from around the world, showing their skills and way of life. At times, it was like living in a museum or a circus. You never knew who you were going to meet while walking into your kitchen.

Sean, who became one of my best friends in the house, was an Englishman in his forties who had worked as a musician and as a policeman in London his whole life. He had brown eyes, a bald head, and a gorgeous English accent. He had lived in Tallinn for over five years, and made his money as a guitar player in bands before he ended up in our hostel. He loved the Estonian culture and how direct and quiet the people were, and hated what he described as the superficial, boring chit-chat in England.

We hit it off immediately. I loved his dark, quirky, English sense humour, and he loved that I challenged his bantering in my American accent. He taught me to play *Wish you were here* and *Tequila!* on the guitar, and gave me advice on how to get over my heartache caused by the young, gel-haired landlord (who, it turned out, opened his door, arms, and pants, to every girl in town).

As two insomniacs, Sean and I would spend countless nights sitting in the upstairs loft, smoking and chatting about life, while I was stroking his grey cat and he drank endless gallons of black tea with milk and sugar.

Even though Estonia had been free for almost 20 years and had made a tremendous step forward from the complicated

Soviet Union/90s' days, Western people still seemed to think of us as a 'poor Russian village country'. When we joined the EU in 2004 and our borders opened to the whole world, Estonia became a notorious place for the English bachelors and their crazy stag parties.

Throughout the 2000s, every Estonian crime or police TV show featured some British men in their episodes every week, and it became something of a joke. It seemed like they thought they were coming to a poor, non-English speaking country, where their accent and money would be so attractive they could get any girl they want. Instead, they ended up being so wasted that they had to spend the night with the police instead.

I have to admit, I never got to know how much a pint of beer cost in a bar, because I never needed to buy one. There were so many Englishmen buying drinks, hoping to get you drunk and then have sex with you, that I never even had to open my wallet when I went out. Not that I was even drinking. I found bantering with them entertaining, and I wasn't a big drinker anyway.

It usually took four beers and two shots for the Englishmen to be so wasted that their talk became incomprehensible, then I could go home to hang out with my favourite Londoner and his grey cat.

After the first semester at university, it became clear to me that my grades were so poor there was no way in hell I could even apply to the Erasmus programme to live and study in France the following year. So I left university and decided I'd go to France on my own.

At that time, I was working in a 24h grocery shop in Tallinn Old Town, getting minimum wage and poor blood circulation from standing up for twelve hours straight. But I only managed to stay there for a month - the work was just too bad, and I was too reckless to care for it. As the spring came along, I took my month's pay and headed to France with a backpack, thinking and hoping this could be my new home. It was time to fulfil my French dream.

I returned ten days later, wishing I could have come back earlier. I felt tired, unimpressed, and sad. Instead of getting a job and working my way up from there, I had been harassed on the streets, gone to Nice to see the famous beach, and come home from there. The only nice person I came across during these ten days was this Norwegian guy I met on the train, who took me out for a pizza and didn't try to put his hands down my pants. Which I really appreciated. Everything else was a complete nightmare and left me confused about my entire life choices.

I returned to the hostel in Tallinn, sad, lost, and confused, not sure what to do with my life. I knew I couldn't stay there longer than another month. Busy summertime was approaching, the whole house was about to change, and the guy of my dreams was spending every night with a new girl, kissing them in front of me.

I didn't know what to do, but I knew I couldn't continue like this. So, I hung out with Sean and his cat in the loft, watching him drinking tea while he watched me falling into sad darkness, night after night after night.

As the summer approached, the hostel got busier and more tourists started coming in. On another insomniac night, when I dragged myself to the upstairs loft to complain to Sean about life and the weirdness of it, I found that he wasn't alone. He was sitting there with a woman from the Isle of Wight named Hannah, who had come to Tallinn for the weekend. Now there were two people drinking black tea with milk and sugar, and me staring at both of them while they talked about all things English.

Sean hadn't been back to England in about three years, and had spent all this time with Estonians, so being able to talk about things back in his former home made him happier and more excited than I had ever seen him. They were both talking about London and its madness in the most romantic way.

"Eva, why don't you go to London?" Sean asked me abruptly. 'France didn't work out, but England would. You already speak the language and you'll get a job easily in London.'

Hannah was next to him, nodding and getting excited. 'Yes, London! You definitely should go there!'

For me, England equalled rainy days, an expensive lifestyle, people drinking cups of teas and eating fish and chips, occasionally bantering like they do in *Never Mind the Buzzcocks* TV show (which I've loved since I was a young teenager), while whining about the weather. Somewhere, there was the Queen sitting on her golden throne talking in her fancy English accent, eating scones and drinking milky tea.

I had always loved English bands – the Rolling Stones, David Bowie, Arctic Monkeys, the Kooks, Queen, Amy Winehouse – but all this beauty had been darkened by the wasted lads I had seen in Tallinn with bad teeth and worse manners, drunkenly screaming: "I COME FROM ENGLAND, OKAY, LOVE? DO YOU SPEAK ENGLISH? IS YOU ALRIGHT? HOW MUCH MONEY? YES, YOU. YOU, HOW MUCH?"

That was England for me. I had seen my fair share of English lads right here in Tallinn, and I couldn't have cared less about the Queen, tea, or rain.

"Nah, I don't really care for England, to be honest. I don't have enough money to go live in an overpriced city, anyway," I told them.

They insisted I go to England nevertheless.

"You've wanted to go away for a while now, and London is the best option. You speak the language, you understand the humour, and you'll find work with no problem. The English are very pretentious and don't want to do a lot of jobs. That's why there's so many immigrants in London. There's just so many jobs available that the locals themselves don't want to do," Sean explained. "Believe me, the real English lads are much better than the ones you see here in Tallinn."

Hannah was already looking at airline tickets. Ryanair had just started flying there, so the prices were very cheap.

They were more excited and confident about my future than I was. There was nothing in me that wanted to go to England. Years before, I had known a girl whose father worked as a lorry driver in Europe and had to go to England every now and again. He said that he tried to avoid going to the UK as much as he could, because he was tired of constantly being told off for not being able to speak Russian or Polish. "But Estonia is just a little village in Russia, innit? You all speak Polish and Russian, innit!? No? Fuck off!"

I really was not interested in being spoken to like that.

Our little English party was interrupted by the boy who I had been dreaming of that whole year and who was the only reason I had come to live in this hostel. He rocked up with a girl and a bottle of bubbly, sat down on one of the couches, opened the bottle, and started making out with the girl who could barely stand up. I wanted to die.

Sean and Hannah kept talking about their English food and lives, while my crush was about to create a new one with some random bird in front of me. I looked at him, then I looked at Sean. I was a second away from screaming at the lovers or crying in front of them.

So I took a deep breath, the last that was left in my broken body, and said as loud as I could, "Fuck it! Yeah, maybe I should go! Yeah, why not! Screw it, let's go to London!"

I tried to sound enthusiastic about this newfound plan, whereas I was actually hoping that my crush would hear my words through all his kissing, leave the girl, and confess his eternal love for me on the spot. But he didn't. He was too busy examining this random girl's tonsils with his tongue, and nothing else existed for him at that moment... especially me.

There I was, trying to catch my love's attention with a shivering voice, and a second away from crying. But Sean and Hannah heard me.

"Yes! Yes, London is going to be great! And you must visit me in the Isle of Wight," she said.

"Nah, Isle of Wight is too far. She's gonna be a Londoner from now on," Sean said confidently, giving me a proud, cheeky smile.

I was not feeling confident nor smiley at all. I was still hoping my love would hear me and be interested in me, instead of this girl. I had said the words out loud about going to London, but I did not really believe them.

"Only on one condition, though,' I announced. 'I will not go by myself. If I find somebody to go there with – anybody – then I will go. But I'm not gonna go there alone."

Going to France had shown me that moving to live in a new country was hard enough, but could be excruciatingly difficult if you did it alone. I needed a partner in crime. I also said it, hoping in a way that I maybe wouldn't have to go at all.

However, I left this choice up to the Universe. If London was written in my stars, the Universe would send someone on my way.

"Sean, go with her. Don't you miss London?" Hannah asked him.

"Hell, no, I will never go back there. I love it here too much," he said immediately. "Plus," he added confidently, sipping his tea and smiling at me, "she'll be just fine there."

I don't know what made him so sure about it all. I felt the total opposite – lost, weird, and uncertain. But hey, I had proposed an ultimatum to the Universe, and frankly, I thought it was too much to become real. So there was no reason to actually worry about it. My bigger problem was the man kissing the wrong woman, in front of me.

Hannah stayed in the hostel for another two days, spending all her time telling me the best places in London, where to go, what to do, how to be, England this, and England that. She was so happy that I was going to go to her home country, even though I didn't have a ticket nor did I show any excitement over the possible move. I was still holding on to my ultimatum with the Universe. I'd washed my hands of the worrying that comes with planning, and was allowing the Universe do its work if this move was meant to be.

The only good thing that came out of my 24h grocery shop days was my colleague, Lemmi. She was determined to go to Australia (she even had the visa and everything), and we had bonded instantly when she'd found out I was planning to go to France. But we'd only worked two shifts together, exchanged numbers, and then I had left.

A few days after my supposed deal with the Universe, she suddenly texted me. We hadn't seen each other for over a month.

"How's France? All good?" she asked.

"Screw France. I'm back home but thinking about going to London. How's Australia?" I texted her back.

"I don't know if I want to go to Australia any more. But London is boring and has crappy salaries, why would you wanna go there?"

Lovely! Looked like the whole world was confused and uncertain of what was about to happen. I didn't have an answer for her.

A day later, she sent me another text: "Do you want to go to London with me?"

Cards had been dealt. The universe had shown me their hand, now it was my turn to show my ace. It was like the game Leonardo DiCaprio played before getting on the *Titanic*. That one game that determined Jack's future.

It looked like I had just won the tickets. To what? To a country that was gonna kill me slowly yet determinedly, without even an option of a random floating door?

I was almost ready to text Lemmi back that I was not going anywhere and would stay in Estonia, where I belong. I had no intention of going to England – a country full of tea-sipping queens who expect me to speak Russian or Polish and would get angry at me for not knowing either – with a girl I'd only met twice in my life. I really wanted to tell her all of that.

But then I heard the guy of my dreams going upstairs with a new random bird, laughing and kissing between the incredibly hilarious jokes he was apparently telling. Every step they took on those stairs felt like a stomp on my already fragile heart. And when the loft door made its quirky opening sound, I knew I had had enough. I was not gonna go upstairs any more and watch the same shitshow I had done many, many times before just to be closer to him. This time, I was drawing the line. I was getting out. I was done.

"Sure, let's go to London. Let's buy the tickets tomorrow?" I texted Lemmi.

"Let's do this," she texted me back.

Lemmi came to mine the next day and we bought the tickets to London. Hand luggage only. One way only. Gatwick Airport was apparently a good place to go (or so they said).

We had ten days to cut all ties with the life we had created so far and make plans for the next one.

She was determined never to return to Estonia. "Things are not right, I don't like it here," she told me. She had lived and worked in Finland before, so was used to moving and living abroad.

And me? I had nothing to lose; no ties to cut. All of my childhood friends were doing different things, going to university, living their own lives. The friends I had made during this year in the hostel were citizens of the world, constantly travelling and living by the wind.

I called my mom and told her I wouldn't be returning to Pärnu for a while. 'Okay,' was her answer. My grandmother said the same. No questions asked, just like a real Estonian.

Sean gave me a big smile and a hug once I told him that I was leaving. In the most confident and proud voice, he assured me I would get along just fine and find a job easily. I smiled back nervously.

My crush was right there; this time, sober and without anybody on his lap. He looked at me in a strange way. "So, you're really leaving?"

"Uhuh." Actually, I wanted to throw myself in his arms and never let him go. If he would have said *anything* at that moment, I would have stayed. But the nice shirt he was wearing gave me a hint that the man was going out to have another great night with some other woman. One I did not want to hear anything about. One I was running away from.

'I'm leaving in ten days.' More nervous laughter, trying to look confident. *Try to look happy for this choice you just made, even if you feel like it's the biggest mistake of your life,* I told myself. He was looking at me strangely, while I tried to hold onto the little self-esteem and fake confidence I had left in me.

His face never gave away any of his emotions, nor was he ever gonna say what he felt. Like a true Estonian.

The men in England better speak, I thought angrily, *because I've had enough of mysterious looks, mind games and unspoken words! England better be full of those happy, fun people I had once seen in those music videos as a child!*

Ah, who was I kidding? I had already learned that life wasn't like those videos anywhere. Nobody was gonna sing or dance or be as pretty and happy as they were on TV, even if I travelled the world fifty times over.

The reality was that I knew I was gonna be living in a huge metropolis, and be just another immigrant running away from something in their home country, ready to do any job just to get by and argue for my right to exist with the natives.

But hey, at least I wouldn't have to hear about *his* love life any more. And no matter what shit was gonna be thrown at my way, it wouldn't hurt more than the pain of unrequited love.

ACT I

~

THE BEGINNING

2

~

MY FLIGHT TO LONDON WAS AT 7AM, and I was so excited and scared that I stayed up all night.

I went to see Sean before I left. His life in the hostel was going to change, too, because of the busy tourist season ahead. He was enjoying one of the last quiet, insomniac nights with the girl he had spent all winter with.

He was so excited and happy that I was going. 'You're gonna do so well,' he kept repeating with his warm cheeky smile. 'Say that you know "very nook and cranny" of this place; it's an old English saying,' he advised.

'Nook and cranny? Uhuh,' I repeated, trying to think of anything other than England, planes, or the morning ahead.

'Nook and cranny, nook and cranny,' he kept saying. He taught me other phrases as well that were supposedly very English and would make me sound cool. But unfortunately they all fell on death ears. I was busy trying to hold myself in one piece.

It was half five when Lemmi called me to come downstairs where she was waiting in the cab.

I took my small backpack with a few clothes and a note-book, then left my keys on the table and closed the door behind me. It was early in the morning but the sun was already so strong it was burning my skin. Farewell, sunny days; hello, rainy, grey England.

As I got on that plane, I refused to let myself think too much about what the future held. Frankly, I wouldn't have been able to step on the plane if I had given it a thought. I fastened my seatbelt and kept my eyes on Lemmi, who was as joyful as a wind-up toy, dancing, smiling, and singing how we were gonna be in London soon. I refused to think of the reality.

Even though I was scared to death, I was also excited. A little part of me wanted to see how much I could endure, and I had some sort of belief in me that this could work out. At least I knew where we were gonna stay that evening; I had arranged for us to couch surf in some French guy's place. After that, I was ready for anything.

Having lived in a hostel for almost a year, I had seen how people always manage to get by and survive somehow. I also had Lemmi with me, and even though we didn't really know each other, she was so cheerful and thrilled that whenever I was in doubt, I looked at her excited face and thought to myself, *We'll be fine*.

Although time would come to show that the definition of the word 'fine' means different things to different people, I can say, in hindsight, that we were going to be fine. We *were* fine. But in very, very different ways.

Unbeknown to me, Lemmi had also done her research. She had contacted this Estonian guy that was living in Lewisham, who was supposed to help us with moving into a new town. His name was Roland, he was only 17, rode BMX bikes, and was supposedly very cool. We spent the first day together and he showed us around town, helping us buy Oyster cards and a brick phone with a new SIM card. We taught him new Estonian slang words in return. He hadn't spoken Estonian in such a long time, so it was funny to hear his accent and ancient use of words.

Roland had come to London a few years earlier to live with his mother. I never found out the specifics about when, why, or how. To be honest, me and him didn't exactly become best friends, though he and Lemmi got along very well. Very, very well. They were dating by the second week we were there.

From that first day onwards, Roland was hanging out with us at all times, unless he had to go to school. In Estonia, summer vacation starts early June and finishes on the 1st of September, but as I found out, the English spend half of their summer in school. That must be horrible. But luckily for me, it meant I could hang out with Lemmi without Roland constantly being all over her.

Roland knew a woman in Lewisham who was renting out one of her bedrooms for some extra cash. It wasn't bad, but we tried to get out of there as soon as possible. It's not easy living in a family house, especially if the family isn't yours.

Even though our arrival day had been very sunny and warm, June 2011 turned out to be very cold, rainy, and dark – both in weather and the path of our new lives. I knew England was the country of rain, but I hadn't expected it to be that bad.

My first weeks in London were horrible, to say the least. All my plans started to fail me immediately, and the confidence, hope, and social skills I had gained in the hostel began to fade. I felt like a little awkward child in a big adult concrete world. Hard as concrete were the high buildings and never-ending streets; cold as concrete were the hearts, words, and the looks of the millions of people living in it. I felt like the only nice English person in this world was Sean, whose friendliness had lured me into his world. Unfortunately, he was thousands of miles away, and I was stuck in a land of rude, cold, and very unfriendly people, who were nothing like him.

Although London is one of the greenest cities in the world, it had nothing on my home, which was like a fairyland in the middle of forests. People's houses. All brown. All semi-detached/detached. All looking the same. Like copy and paste, copy and paste, only to be interrupted by trees or abandoned looking areas. No wonder so much great punk and sad rock comes from the UK; I'd be a sad rebel, too, if I had to call this grey, isolated existence my home.

When you ask, what did I expect to see – skyscrapers and big city lights? My answer is yes; that is exactly what I expected to see. Throughout my whole life, I had read and understood from the Western media and the British stag party lads how everything in eastern European was poor, horrible, and depressing. I was surprised to find that their own buildings and environment gave me suicidal thoughts faster than anything in my previous life.

Then there were the people: everybody rushing somewhere, fighting for their existence, nobody had time, money, or energy. Their actions were harsh and indifferent, although they sugar-coated it with fake politeness: "How are you? So nice to meet you! I am so sorry. Miss you! Sorry, sorry, sorry!" Sorry should be every Englishman's second name, because they use it constantly yet rarely with any real meaning.

I guess, though, it was my own fault for believing those words. For example, when people asked me how I was, I really did think they wanted to know about my life and how I felt lost. I also foolishly believed them when they said sorry, yet stepped on my feet again and elbowed me in the ribs on the tube. I learned, quite reluctantly but quite fast, that the right answers to these two phrases are always (I repeat: ALWAYS): 'I'm good!' and 'Sorry!' And I've never meant anything more in my life.

It didn't take me and Lemmi long to understand that our understanding of a good home, respectable job, and what we held important, were quite different. I didn't mind living anywhere, as long as it was cheap; hostel life had made me quite tolerant of anything. But Lemmi was more ambitious work-wise, and needed a really good, clean place to live.

So, my plan of working and living in hostels was out, if I wanted to be with her. And I did want to be with her. We were obviously going to follow different lives, but at that moment, both of our paths were still too fragile to be walked alone. She had lived in Finland before, so she knew the formula of leaving home and starting new somewhere else. Yet London was too much to handle alone, even for her. I, on the other hand, was too naive and carefree to be alone in a country that felt so cold, rigid, and abusive. So, we stayed together.

Things also didn't work out job-wise. We would walk around with our CVs and talk to people every day, but with no luck. Everybody's first question (and sometimes the only question) was whether I had any work experience in England. 'No, I only arrived here four days ago' was not a good enough answer for them.

Frankly, nobody gave a toss about our CVs. Unfortunately for me, I didn't know how to lie back then. I didn't know how to sell myself, and didn't want to believe I had to pretend to be somebody or something else in order to get something. How stupid and naive of me.

'Sorry love, good luck,' was usually their answer. Oh yes, I also learned that people can call you 'darling' and 'love' while actually thinking you're a piece of crap. As a matter of fact, they most definitely think you're a piece of crap when they condescendingly call you 'darling'. That, unfortunately, took me longer to learn.

So, when anybody called me 'darling' or 'love' during my first four months in England, my little sad heart and utterly foolish head sparked up and fell a bit in love with them, too.

Weeks went by, each one more miserable than the other, as Lemmi and I ran around London looking for work and being constantly disappointed. Sean's words 'You'll get a job easily, there's so many jobs English don't want to do so they'll give it to the immigrants' rang through my head, and I wondered where those jobs were. I was looking for them everywhere but still found nothing. At that moment, anything sounded great; anything would do.

We reckoned we must really suck if nobody wanted to hire us even in the summer – one of the busiest periods of the year. We were both depressed and felt defeated.

Lemmi's way of dealing with defeat was to go to Superdrug and Boots, buy all sorts of make-up, and accessorize herself. She was a beautiful, tiny girl with a great body, who knew all the secrets of make-up. Her face was a canvas on which she painted her moods every morning, and she looked flawless – her eyebrows, foundation, eyes, lips, and cheeks, as well as her hair, clothes, shoes. She also had a great singing voice, and her favourite music was East Side old school hip-hop, which she listened to daily to bump her up for possible job interviews.

While Lemmi did her everyday morning make-up routine, while singing to Biggie Smalls, I was usually still half asleep. I had short hair, baggy clothes, a careless personality and, to top it all off, I was much taller than Lemmi. When we were walking around town, I looked more like her entourage than a friend. The only indicator of my female sex was my curvy ass that couldn't have possibly belonged to any man.

Me and Lemmi were as different from each other, both in appearance and personality, as two people can be. The only thing that tied us together was the unknown, and fear of an unfamiliar future.

'You'd get a job more easily if you wore make-up. I'm sure you'd get hired if you cleaned yourself up a bit and looked more like a girl,' Lemmi would tell me daily. To be honest, she wasn't lying. I did look like a goofy Hungarian sheepdog trying to mould itself into some human form. On the other hand, she looked like a Greek goddess, but was still unemployed, too.

The first and the most promising offer I finally got was from a shoe shop in Camden. After walking around unsuccessfully for two weeks in a row, soaked each time (umbrellas from the Poundland didn't really help), this woman agreed to give me a trial shift at the shoe shop. I felt amazing, I felt invincible. Was my luck finally turning around?

The next day, I got to Camden nice and early. Clean clothes, clean hair. I was at my best, ready to learn and work hard. That woman wasn't. She said she had forgotten that I was even supposed to come. My heart dropped.

Hoping to still get a job, I spent a whole day fixing shoeboxes downstairs in the dark, smelly basement, along with an Asian girl and a Bangladeshi boy. They knew even less than me, both work and language-wise.

Unfortunately for me, I didn't know my rights at that time. A trial shift can't legally last for more than four hours, unless they want to pay you. I spent a whole day downstairs amongst stinking shoes, without a break or any advice. And at the end of the day, the woman told me 'sorry' and wished me good luck for the future. I had heard the words 'sorry' and 'good luck' so many times in those couple of weeks that I wanted to vomit and cry at the same time.

I thought about my crush back in Tallinn a lot. I was sure he was making out with every girl in town on the sunny beaches of Estonia while I was stuck in some big city's basement shoe shops and not even getting paid for it.

I cried so much during my first month in England that I didn't even mind the constant rain. As a matter of fact, it gave me a good excuse when people said, 'Why do you look so miserable and shit? Oh, you got caught in the rain? Fair enough. Sorry, though, love. Good luck with some other job!' Lovely.

3

~

I had come to London with about £900. It was all the money I had saved up since the Fourth Grade (when I knew my future was to be a poor immigrant in a big city and could do with some help). Every penny of lunch money I had kept, every kroon I had gotten for my birthdays, had only roughly made £900 after the currency exchange. Actually, I found it to be a reasonable sum of money, but after two weeks of unsuccessful job searches, I grew restless.

London is not exactly a place where you can hang out and enjoy the scenery. Let's be honest, there is absolutely nothing to look at in this city – just heaps of buildings, one after another, grey sky, Meal Deal packages lying around on street corners, and heaps of people all rushing somewhere. There is the River Thames – and rivers are always nice – but apparently it's so infested with diseases and bacteria that one of the first things I learned in London was never to touch that water unless I wanted to die, which at times was very tempting.

It was quite comforting to know that if I did not get a job in this city and fell so deep into depression, then all I had to do was walk into the Thames and all the bacteria would eat me quickly enough.

Lemmi and I weren't getting along well, yet we needed each other in order to pay cheap rent and to have a shoulder to cry on. So, I was pretty restless. And worried about the future.

One evening, I came very close to walking into the river, when I went to withdraw money for rent and was baffled to see I only had £200 left. That meant I could only pay rent for another two weeks if I didn't eat or do anything else. After that, I would have no money. Like, zero.

I couldn't call my grandmother or my mother and tell them about my situation, because it had been my decision to come to this country. I had dug my own hole and it was my duty to drag myself out of it. I knew that calling them would mean three minutes of being told off, with comments like, 'All your friends are in uni, and where are you? In a foreign country where nobody, obviously, NOBODY wants you nor likes you, so what are you doing there? You must come back now and stop this circus. Be like a normal person.' They loved that word 'circus'. Most of the things I did reminded them of a ridiculous, stupid circus.

I couldn't bear to hear it. I already felt low enough, and had a condescending voice inside me that kept putting me down daily. Loud, aggressive, patronizing, it was mocking me for the dream of living abroad and for thinking I could ever make it.

That's why Lemmi and I stuck together, despite our differences. We were two fragile trees that felt lost and depressed, but we could manage to get through another day by leaning on each other. When one started falling, the other held her up, saying words of encouragement and hope, even when she didn't believe them herself. And vice versa.

I withdrew the last £200 I had, gave away the £100 for another week's rent for a place I hated, and spent another £5 on the internet cafe, where I promised myself I wouldn't leave until I found myself a job. I started to understand that the rules I had learned and seen in Estonia would not apply here. Believing in the kindness of strangers and just going with the flow would not work in this country. In order to survive, I had to have a game plan. I had to be, or at least pretend to be, stronger than I was and just push through. And I had to do it now.

Right. £95 left. Let's go.

There was an internet shop on the Lewisham high street that we'd usually go to apply for jobs and to have any sort of interaction with the world we had left behind. I would stalk my friends on Facebook and look at their pictures of sunbathing on Estonia's beaches, all tanned and happy. I hadn't seen sunshine in about three weeks by that point, and was so white I was starting to look transparent. They would ask how I was and I'd answer, 'Good. It's a bit hard, but it's alright.' They'd reply how cool it must be to be in London, but I didn't tell them how I cried and fantasized about my death every day. Instead, I sent them a smiley face.

If there was anything London had taught me by that stage, it was to suck it up, put a smile on your face, and stop whining. People are too busy with their problems; they really don't have time to put up with anyone else's.

With the help of Google, I fixed my CV (aka, learned how to lie better) and sent it everywhere. I made a big deal about what a great salesperson I had been in Camden, how amazing my customer skills were, and how much I loved putting shoes on people's feet. They didn't have to know that I had actually only done a trial shift and spent it in the basement, kept away from all the customers. Everybody lies on their CV, anyway.

By the end of the second day, I got a call from a hotel who thanked me for applying to their job and invited me to a trial the next day.

'Sure,' I said. 'I'll be there.' I had no idea what the caller was talking about. Had I applied for a job at a hotel? What type of a job? What hotel?

The next day, I put on my best clothes (aka, the least baggy and dirty ones) and went up north, past Camden. North

London felt completely different to south London; the streets were cleaner, and there were no chicken and chip shops. I was very surprised how one city could have so many different parts to it.

It turned out that I had applied to an agency that was providing workers for big, fancy hotels. I had never heard of agencies, so I didn't know what kind of work I was going to do, but I said yes to everything they offered me because I needed the money. What other option did I have? Go back to Estonia and prove to my family that I was, indeed, a talentless, miserable human being that gets nothing done? Not yet.

I knew I could endure more, and I wanted to see what else was going to happen. I felt like I couldn't go any lower than I already was (well, getting killed, raped, or both, would have been cherry on top of my already shit cake), so I decided to try everything.

It was the early morning of 23rd of June when I went to the hotel to find out what my job was going to be. In Estonia, 23rd of June is a bank holiday – Jaanipäev. It's a nice tradition that started when Estonia won a battle on that day in 1917, and was a major accomplishment towards our first independence the following year. Nowadays, Estonian people celebrate it by going to the countryside, getting wasted, jumping over bonfires, and eating shitloads of BBQ, while singing and dancing to horrible, traditional drinking songs. Since it's the whitest night of the year (which up in the north means about 22-23 hours of daylight), everybody stays up, staggering around the good old country roads for a day or two, without any recollection of whether the night has already been and gone or has still to come.

My heart heavy and my head still confused with unrequited love, I went to see what I had signed myself up. It turned out that my job was to be a cleaner in a prestigious hotel in Knightsbridge. There was me and another four girls, and we all looked as if we had no idea what we had gotten ourselves into.

A woman gave us leaflets of what everything meant in English, with pictures. For example, there was a picture of a pillow: 'This is a pillow', 'This is a bed', 'This is a man, and this is a woman'.

Oh my God. I felt like I was back in the Second Grade. I had been a little bit hesitant about my English language skills before arriving in London, thinking that they weren't good enough, but after three weeks in England I was surprised to be given leaflets explaining the basic English words. I did not know what to think, and started to doubt my own knowledge.

To my amazement, the other girls were very happy to be given such colourful leaflets, and were commenting enthusiastically on the picture with a woman in PJs. I couldn't believe this was my real life. But what else could I do? I needed the money, as I only had about £80 left on my card. And the last three weeks had shown me that no matter what I did, nobody gave me any work.

They didn't mind I didn't have NANO (whatever that was supposed to be) and that I didn't know my full address (I still didn't understand the whole postcode AND street names thing). They just wanted somebody to work. And I just needed some money. So we signed the contract.

As I was walking home that day, all I could think about was my family and friends opening up their first drinks, grilling BBQs, driving to the countryside, setting up the big fireplaces, and getting ready to dance, eat, and sing on the whitest night of the year. My crush would probably shag ten women. Everybody would be happy, the whole country in harmony.

What was I about to do? It felt like I had signed my soul to the devil and had no way out of there. I went to bed at 10pm in preparation to be up by 6am. It was dark and rainy outside, and I wanted to die.

My amazing work experience at the prestigious hotel lasted for exactly ten days, yet my admiration for cleaners and the realization of how hard their job actually is will last forever. Seriously.

On my first day, I was put together with a woman who had worked there for eleven years. All day long she was supposed to show, talk, and explain to me how everything was done and in what order, but instead she was silent the whole time we were scrubbing the mirrors or doing the beds. I could only guess that she was probably numb from all the shit she had seen (literally and figuratively), and couldn't have cared less about life any more.

The whole point of cleaning is that you get about ten rooms to do in about eight hours. If you follow a certain way of doing everything and the supervisor is fine with your work, you can be finished even faster and go home earlier. And you also get a nice, hot meal for lunch (at least we did). Sounds simple, doesn't it?

Well, the next few days that I was there proved to me that it's pretty hard. I managed to do about five rooms in nine hours. There were days I didn't even go and have my delicious lunch because I was too behind schedule and too stressed to eat. I thought I did a good job until the supervisor would come, scream at my apparent incompetence, rip everything apart, and make me do it all again. Next room, same thing. Third room, same thing.

My biggest obstacle was the bed. They gave me rooms that always had queen-sized beds. Lucky me; I had only slept in single beds my whole life, and until working in this hotel,

I didn't even know beds that big existed. I must admit, changing duvets that were three times my size turned out to be a very complicated process for me. Every time I tried to change the duvet, I got lost in it, and half suffocated myself in those enormous sheets. Once I did manage to get the duvet done, you also had to add those little beauty bits to make the bed look extra fluffy and gorgeous, which basically sent me into a frenzy. I started seeing those beds like battlefields that I tried to avoid at any cost.

It got so bad that by the sixth day the supervisor yelled at me so loud the whole floor could hear us.

'How is it possible not to know how to do a bed? Where is your home? How do you live?'

People staying at the hotel with fancy Louis Vuitton travel bags would give me frightened, uncomfortable looks and walk quickly by. Other cleaners would look at me with scared eyes and run back to their rooms to make sure their beds were immaculate. She then made sure I never worked on her floor again.

Every morning, I would wake up at 6am and drag my sad, sleepy ass to Gloucester Road to work with chemicals that had big labels on them, saying how harmful they were for the environment. They had pictures of dead fish and trees on them, to make them look extra creepy. I worked with those things without any gloves or anything, so I am amazed I still have any fingerprints left. They smelt great, even though I knew that sitting in that little chemical cloud was also killing my brain cells and probably making me addicted to sniffing glue. But I did it anyway.

Around 5pm, I would drag that same sad ass back home on an overcrowded tube train, which felt like a mission in itself. I have never felt more like a slave to the wage than I do when I'm standing in the queue for the next train at rush hour, and everybody's sweaty, tired, and frustrated bodies are fighting for some oxygen and space left in the underground. Politeness has a different meaning for those 2.5 hours that the rush hour lasts; humanity doesn't exist. Everybody has had to pretend to be a cheerful, professional human being for eight (or more) hours straight that day already, so they can't be bothered to do more of it on the tube. That means it's every man for themselves. If you're pregnant, disabled, or elderly, please – for the love of God, and your own sake – avoid the rush hours on London underground trains.

After standing up for nine hours at work, I had to stand for another hour on the tube. Sometimes it would be fine and the trains were so packed that I could lean on strangers and put less pressure on my legs. But other times I would be so tired and my legs so weak that I didn't even care about everybody staring at me as I sat down on the floor. I think other people is the last thing on your mind when your body feels like it's shutting down from exhaustion. And mine felt constantly like that.

The only person who understood my frustration was Lemmi. She had worked as a cleaner in Finland some years before, so she knew how tough the job could be and didn't judge me for feeling like a zombie, both physically and mentally. She was still struggling to find work herself, despite applying for many jobs every day.

She actually had a trial day at the same hotel, but she walked out on the first day. I don't blame her. It was one messed-up place, and she was smart enough not be lured in by the sweet toxic scent of the chemicals like me. But she also had more money saved up than I did.

I have to admit, the only good thing about being a cleaner (there's probably more, but for me this was the only silver lining in this shit-filled occupation) is that you lose weight while eating whatever you want. Goddamn, I could feel myself shrinking in just those ten days. You can eat a whole roast and all the sweets you can find, yet you've got to be so quick at this work that it'll all come out of you in a few hours, I swear.

Despite having an English bank account, I got my first pay as a cheque for £380 for those ten days I had worked for them. I remember that sum like my life depended on those numbers (well, it kinda did). When I had worked in the 24h shop in Tallinn, I had made €380 in a month, but in England I had earned the same or even more in just ten days! I was so happy I didn't know what to do, so I called my grandmother to tell her the great news.

'Grandma, I just made my first money in England – £380! This is great!' I almost hyperventilated into the phone, still looking at the cheque in disbelief that this money was mine to spend. I didn't tell her the job I had done to get it, nor did she ask. She would have not liked her dear granddaughter to be some random cleaner, as all the immigrants around the world seem to be. It isn't anybody's dream job, even though we all enjoy the benefits of it.

'Ahah,' was her answer. 'I'm busy right now.' And she hung up.

Estonians don't really show many emotions, but I knew this was her way of saying congratulations and being happy for my accomplishment. Even though she hated the fact that I was far away from home (probably somewhere like Auschwitz), doing God knows what, at least the girl got paid for it!

I cashed in the money, feeling like a real gangster in some Hollywood film (because they always go to banks to cash cheques), and let myself be content for the first time in London. I had bought myself a few more weeks in this city.

The money was worth all the pain and stress of the last ten days, even though I had a constant burning and tingling sensation in my fingertips, my ankles were swollen from standing up too long, and I kept having migraines (due to stress, fatigue, malnutrition and perhaps the toxic fumes I liked/was forced to smell at work).

Despite the money and all the beautiful side-effects, I decided to quit the cleaning job few days later. My body was tired, and the idea of walking into that hotel again sent me into a frenzy. I'm sure the decision was mutually welcomed.

Lemmi finally got a job at a wrap/sandwich shop in Soho. And after constant rain throughout the whole of June, it was finally a sunny day. That evening, we drank beer, because we were, for the first time in this city, hopeful about the future – even though I had just quit my job and didn't know what was ahead of me. But I guess that's the effect sunshine has on people – you just feel happier, more hopeful, and better once it comes out. I learned later how the English can handle exactly three days full of sun before they start whining about the weather again. But it's the same with Estonians. However, the first day of sunshine felt almost like a miracle. And I was very happy.

The rent was £100 a week, which meant if I ate very little, I could survive another three weeks. In a few days, I was supposed to go to Estonia for a week for my friend's wedding, and I did consider that I might not return to London, despite having a ticket. For six weeks in a row, I had been nothing but miserable, had no job, and no money, so what was the point in coming back? Perhaps I should do what society said: shut up, go to uni, then get married, instead of running around in this crazy big city that constantly showed its evil, mean side to me. I wouldn't run after a man who beat me up, so why was I letting this city do that to me now?

Lemmi's job turned out to be in the heart of Soho, next to 'some cool jazz bar' (that later turned out to be the world-famous Ronnie Scott's jazz bar, duh!), with some cool young Hungarian boys. The best thing about the job was that she could eat as many wraps and sandwiches as she wanted – and that we both did. I survived that week on chilli beef wraps, to the point that I had a ring of fire. And to mix it up, with some cheap chocolate from Aldi, that made my already sensitive teeth hurt.

I had been away for a month-and-a-half when I returned to Estonia for my friend's wedding. I put on my best dress, washed my hair, and even let Lemmi put some make-up on me so that I'd look good. The moment I got to Tallinn, I went to the hostel to see my old friends – and my crush, of course.

'You alright?' I asked Sean, after a long hug. Roland had taught us the street English, explaining that instead of saying 'hello', you needed to ask, 'you alright?' Roland always taught us the cool, hip things one should say in English in order to sound like a local.

'Yes, I am fine,' was Sean's answer. Then we just stared at each other. His expression was quizzical, my face was confused. In my head, I had expected him to say, 'Yeah, mate, you alright?' So, why did he answer me that he was fine? Who cared how he was? I was saying hello to him in his own mother tongue, not asking him about his actual feelings, wasn't I? Fuck you, Roland. You taught me bullshit.

This went on for a bit. He didn't understand why I wanted to make sure he was alright, and I didn't understand why he didn't understand I was saying hello to him in his own slang.

'Yo, you already seen the Queen yet?' asked my other friends who were still in town. 'No? What else is there to do?'

Well, I didn't want to tell them I spent most of my days trying not to let my depression kill me completely. For a week, I had also scrubbed shit and got yelled at for not knowing how to make a bed. I'd also spent a day in a smelly basement sorting out shoes, without getting anything for it. All is good, though; the toxic fumes I breathe in make me feel dreamy and weightless for a while. Life is great in big, old London town!

I don't know why I couldn't tell my friends the truth. I knew they would've understood and not judged me. Nevertheless, I couldn't say out loud that I was failing. My dream of living abroad, the one I'd had for as long as I could remember, was the one thing I'd always held onto when my life was falling apart. But it had turned out to be one big lie, and a massive failure for me. Saying it out loud would've meant me accepting defeat and giving in, and I did not want to see the ugly truth.

So, I put on a good smile, played the beautiful lie, and listened as my friends said I looked good in my outfit. The dress had cost me £8, and although it meant I couldn't buy food that day, I'd known it would make me look good in front of my desired man. And, by the way, it did. That evening was one of the only times he ever paid attention to me.

I couldn't tell the truth to my family, but I couldn't lie to them either. I spent the whole week crying, only to be interrupted by the wedding (where I cried tears of joy, or so I'd like to think). In fact, I cried so much that my mom got sick of me and told me to figure my life out ASAP. My grandmother had been brought up in the USSR, which meant that any type of strong emotion, besides patriotism or working hard, did not exist in her dictionary. She did not know what to do with this emotional twenty year-old girl. My little sisters were too young to comprehend this messed-up, sad human, and my older sister was being the good Samaritan – going to uni, learning biology, being useful in life, doing what had to be done. I was her exact opposite.

'What should I do?' I asked her, hoping to hear some encouraging words that would give me the energy to keep going.

'Who gives a fuck?' was her answer, just as it had been when we were kids. 'Just try not to die, alright?'

The last sentence showed me that she did love me, Estonian-style. Nevertheless, I cried more.

Yeah, my life in London sucked. All the horror stories my great-grandmother's alcoholic friends had warned me about as a TV-addicted child had turned out to be true: 'These lands are for the rich and famous, not for us. Nobody wants us there. Everybody and everything will be against you.'

Alright then. But if everything was that bad in London, what was the other option? Stay in Estonia? Change my life-long dreams?

Truth be told, Estonia was just as depressing as London. My family members were off in four different directions, everybody doing their own thing. The hostel wasn't the same as it had been before I left; some of my friends had already gone, while others were about to leave the following week. All my childhood friends were doing their own thing, figuring themselves out independently.

Frankly, I felt just as hollow, confused, sad, and miserable when I was back at 'home' as I did when I was 'thousands of miles away'. I had nothing, nowhere.

When I was younger, I used to have a lot of hobbies. I would dance, do gymnastics, row, paint, you name it. Apparently, I've been told, I was a pretty talented kid with a bright future ahead of me. So what happened? I started listening to punk rock, cut off all my hair, began to wear baggy clothes, and quit all my hobbies. Within a year, my so-called bright future turned into a dark presence, with no ambition to change.

'You give up so easily,' my mother would constantly tell me throughout my teenage years.

'You had such a promising future ahead of you, yet you decided to let it all go. Why? If only you had waited a bit longer, held on a bit more…' my grandmother would repeatedly say.

'…You'd probably be very successful now,' my mother would add.

And together they would lower their heads, and their sad eyes would wander off to a better world where their grand-daughter/daughter would be a successful, decent human being. They'd take a deep, disappointed breath and try to accept the fact that actually she was now a poor, confused soul with no money, no job, and no will to live.

I had to watch this scenario and hear those condescending sighs every time those two women happened to be in the same room as me. It was bad enough to hear and see it from them, especially when the same words and images already ran through my mind daily. But I knew that if I returned to Estonia, I would just add fuel to the already burning fire of failures. And I simply couldn't do it.

I went back to London few days later. Crying, as usual. Confused, as usual. Broke, as usual.

It was Lemmi's birthday when I arrived – 18th of July. I was happy to arrive to an empty room so that I could be more miserable by myself, while she was out celebrating with her new colleagues. And I did what every good Samaritan does at a desperate moment when they have nothing left to lose: I got down on my knees and prayed. Through my puffy eyes and swollen nose, that was so runny it had bubbles coming out it, I managed to babble out some words.

'Please, Universe, get me out of this mess, because I sure as hell don't know what to do any more. Please send something good my way. I really will grab onto any opportunity given. Please send somebody my way who can help me get back on track. Anybody. Anything. Please. Thanks."

Once again, I gave myself to the Universe and waited for its cards to be dealt. My last pair had been pretty shit, and I was barely hanging in there. I had nothing to give any more, nothing to be. I needed the Joker, the magical black card.

The next deck dealt, though, changed my whole life. And looking back at that time now, I can't even believe myself what I did. But hey, as I said before, I asked for an opportunity and something, anything, to get me back on track… and that it did.

That's how I met Bobby.

4

~

The next day, I had agreed to meet Lemmi at her work so that I could have a free wrap and to keep myself distracted from sadness. Despite having a job, Lemmi wasn't feeling too good, either. She missed her mom and her boyfriend; she'd broken up with him before coming to London, but they'd got back together on Skype the week I was away.

Her 'relationship' with Roland had only lasted for about a month, until she got tired of making out with an underage boy under the covers in the summer. And it seemed like he didn't really mind, as he became busy with modelling. He was 'discovered' in the BMX park, when some guy took black and white pictures of him smoking and staring deeply into the camera, pretending to be pensive. Somebody in some agency loved these pictures of an underage smoker so much that they decided to send him to Japan.

Well done, Roland, I guess. At least somebody was happy. Lemmi and I were so damn messed-up that everything we had initially run away from became our only force for surviving. Fortunately, she had her mom and a loving boyfriend to give her support, and they were planning to come for a visit in August. I, unfortunately, only had my childhood dreams, fading hope, and stubbornness that kept repeating 'There must be more to life than this. There must be more to life than this' to keep me moving on.

Sick of myself and sick of life, I finally decided to make myself look presentable. I washed my hair and made it curly, and even put some make-up on. I wore a long, flowy top instead of my usual baggy, boy clothes. When I met Lemmi for food, she informed me that it was actually a nightgown, not a daytime top, but it was already too late to change. And, frankly, I couldn't have cared less.

Usually, I would never remember what I had been wearing or make such a big deal about my clothes, but on that occasion, I know my appearance changed my life. It was the only reason Bobby started talking to me.

I kept strolling around central London and ended up in Westminster – tourist central. Big Ben, Parliament, and the London Eye have all been crammed into this one place. Its station has about nine exits, and every day hundreds of thousands of people pass this place. It's a perfect area for buskers, painters, magicians, and all sorts of creatives, who want to make a few pounds from the tourists.

On that particular day, I happened to be in the right station, at the right time, at the right exit, listening to the right busker. Bob Marley was being played, my hair was flowing in the summery station draught, and my make-up was doing a great job of hiding my puffy, red eyes. I was walking around aimlessly, trying to get to the other side of the station so that I could continue wandering around.

'Hey, you there! Hey, blondie!'

At first, I didn't hear anything. But then I got stuck in the queue and couldn't move. Next thing I knew, somebody was tapping me on the shoulder. I turned around and met these big, cheerful brown eyes.

'Yes, you! Blondie! How are you? Come here!' He spoke to me like an old lost friend who was so happy to see his buddy again. Gently, yet firmly, he pulled me next to him into his little busking corner, away from the queue, as everybody was rushing past.

'How have you been? How you doing?' he asked enthusiastically, as if he really wanted to know. His big eyes stared deep into my soul.

'Uumm, I'm good…' I murmured, not really understanding what had just happened. But I had learned that the answer to this question is that you're always good, even if you're on your way to commit suicide.

Within a few minutes, he managed to ask me what I was doing, where I was living, and how my life was. To my surprise, I told this new-found friend everything. In one of the most crowded stations in one of the biggest cities in the world, I managed to find myself in a corner, telling my life story to a stranger I had literally only met a minute before.

I surprised myself. Everything just slipped through my lips. It was funny. I hadn't felt that at ease and present in months, and now I was feeling like a zen in the middle of this rush-hour Westminster station corner with a complete stranger.

'Well, if you're struggling with money, you should come live with me! I'm living in Crystal Palace, it's very nice! It's in south London, near Brixton,' he said casually, as though moving in with a stranger you'd randomly met on the metro 60 seconds before was the most logical thing ever.

Brixton? During that month-and-a-half I had lived in London, I had understood that the south side of the city was like Estonia in the 90s – full of crackheads and criminals who would mug and stab you the moment you came out of the station. I had been told that I had been lucky nothing bad had happened to me the night I had stayed in Loughborough Junction, on my first night in this town.

He must have seen the suspicion on my face.

'If you live with me, you don't have to pay rent!' he said slyly, like he was trying to sell life to me.

'Why not? Are you squatting?' I asked.

His face went blank and his eyes got even bigger, as he stared at me in disbelief.

He must have understood that even though I had recently arrived in this city and didn't know its rules yet, I wasn't that oblivious to what went on. I had grown up listening to English punk bands, and had read how most of these musicians lived in abandoned buildings at some point in their lives. Squatting was part of the English culture, which indicated that there was more to the country than the tea-sipping Queen and horny, lager-drinking lads. There were also tea-and-lager-drinking chaps that fought with the authorities for human rights, and sometimes made songs about it.

In one look, he examined me from head to toe as if I was the police. Quickly realising that no cop would wear a night-gown during daytime and look as goofy as I did, he told me confidently to meet him in an hour. Then he took my number on his phone.

'Gotta play while there's people around, but let's grab a drink later,' he said, winking at me. Then he grabbed his guitar and started singing Marley songs that echoed all over the station corridors. Immediately, people started throwing their money into his guitar bag.

'But what is your name?' I had completely forgotten to ask him, our whole conversation had been so easy that it had felt as though I should have known it already.

He smiled and said, while singing, 'My name is Bobby.'

Alright then, Bobby. Nice to meet ya, I thought to myself, then went for a walk around Southbank.

Usually, I would never give my number to strangers, let alone wait for them for an hour. But I felt weirdly good about this one. I mean, what could go wrong? I was already money-less, so there was nothing to steal.

I felt so depressed I didn't even care if he was gonna kill me. I'm not saying it would have been alright if he did, especially when my sister had specifically asked me to not die, but what the hell? *Let's give it a try*, I thought. I had promised to grab every opportunity coming my way, right?

Bobby was a tall, skinny Rastafarian from the Ivory Coast. His dreadlocks were down to his bum, and he always wore a white or green beanie on top of his head, despite the hot July days. His outfits were always colourful or immaculately white, with a broken guitar bag on his back.

Bobby believed in three things: Jah, Bob Marley, and music. He had been busking in the Westminster station for years, and knew all the other performers there. They took turns throughout the day to allow everyone's talent to earn them a few pounds. I never dared to ask his age, but I assumed he was in his forties. I guess I'll never know.

For our first encounter, Bobby took me to a bar in Southbank and, either understanding I had no money or him being a gentleman, bought me a drink – a Pimm's. 'It's an English summer drink, you'll love it,' he said.

He always spoke with great confidence and determination, like he knew everybody's needs, wants, and secrets, even when they didn't themselves. With his long, skinny body and even skinnier, long fingers, he looked like a master of puppets. I looked at him ordering drinks and wondered if I was about to become his newest addition. Oh well, I had nothing to lose.

I saw the bartender putting fruit into the drink and thought to myself, *What kind of an alcoholic soup is this?* My mother would be proud that I was getting my five-a-day, but it felt like being in a pharmacy where they try to hide healthy poison in the sweetest way.

I love Pimm's now and I know it's an English traditional summer drink – I mean, 'Sun's out, Pimm's out!' – but that day I finished the drink only because I was hungry and that pint of lemonade and pieces of fruit gave me enough calories to keep going. Also, I wasn't much of a drinker. The only thing me and Lemmi sometimes sipped on was the Desperados beer, and even that very rarely.

Bobby was nice. He spoke about busking, his love of music and Marley. He told me about his place in Crystal Palace, how it overlooked the whole of London, how the Number 3 bus went all the way to everywhere in the city. And he insisted that Lemmi and I should go and live with him in his flat. Bobby was amazed I knew about squatting, and our mutual love for playing music united us immediately. His eyes lit up when he heard that I, too, wrote songs and played guitar, but only for my own ears.

I had always played music in my life, starting from the punk rock'n'roll days of my teenage years. During the early June days in London, I had bought myself a cheap guitar through Gumtree so that I could release my stress that way. Unfortunately, it didn't get far, as Lemmi said she couldn't listen to 'this out-of-tune shit mumbling' I called making music, so I had to keep it to myself.

'Imagine, if we would live together, we could make music all day! I could be your producer,' Bobby told me. 'I know a lot about the music business and we could do great things together.' He spoke with a calm, thought-through excitement, like he was selling my new dream life to me. I listened, ate the strawberries and cucumbers, and drank this brown lemonade, all the while nodding at whatever he was saying.

As I said, the man knew how to talk. We had only met an hour before, yet weirdly, I felt more connected and closer to him than I had ever felt, for example, with Lemmi. I don't know whether it was the fact that I had become indifferent and numb from all the stress and failure, but I really felt good around him. Although, I was sure the moment he heard my 'shit out-of-tune mumbling' he would never mention his music producing ideas again. I didn't mind, though; I had no plans about becoming the next superstar. I just wanted a warm bed, food, and a steady job, and it looked like he could offer me the first two things.

When I arrived home some time later, I was full of new energy.

'Lemmi! I met this guy, and we can go live with him in Crystal Palace! For once, we don't have to worry about money! He plays music so we can jam with him! We can move in in two weeks!' I was really excited.

Lemmi, however, was not. She had had enough of England and wanted to go back home. After finding out that Crystal Palace is in Zone 4, she didn't even want to hear about it. She was tired of London, the English accent, the shitty food, the hordes of people, and the inconsistency of work, which wasn't great anyway. She had decided to go back in three weeks' time, right after her boyfriend and mom's visit.

Her news came as a shock and I found myself at a cross-roads. What should I do? Go back with her? We had both been constantly burned by this city in the last two months and, honestly, I was exhausted from fighting, too. I had barely any money left, and the only light that was shining in the future was the possibility of living with Bobby and perhaps getting on my feet that way. But I had just met him; I didn't know him; could I trust this stranger? The glue that had kept me together in this mess – Lemmi – was leaving and I wasn't sure I could handle this city by myself.

It was raining again. Lemmi was Skyping with her boyfriend, giggling and happy about going home and making plans for their future. I was staring into the dark sky, listening to the rain. I didn't have anybody to giggle and be romantic with – not in London, nor in Estonia. Nothing and nobody was waiting for me in either country.

If I left now, my mom and grandmother would probably add another regret to their sad, disappointing granddaughter scenario: 'You give up too easily, yes you do. You went to London, things didn't immediately go your way and you quit that, too. Just like everything in your life. Oh, dear, what are you gonna do now when you have nothing left?' I already imagined them asking me.

I thought about the music videos I had watched as a kid, the ones with all the happy people in the big city that had started this damn dream in my stupid head. I should have just kept to Cartoon Network; I would have been much happier now.

Lemmi only had eyes for her laptop screen and the sweet boyfriend on it.

Bobby texted: 'It was nice meeting you today! See you on Sunday!'

It felt nice to be texted for once by somebody else other than stressed-out Lemmi or my confused mother. I felt as though I had made my first friend in England. Friend. England.

Do you know what? Fuck it. Let's go all the way. If I'm meant to fail, so be it. Let's go find something to love and hold, just like everybody else around the world seems to have. Mama, I'm going to Crystal Palace. You'll see – I don't give up easily. You'll see.

'I'm staying here, Lemmi,' I interrupted her love session.

She looked at me with a concerned look. 'Really? Oh well, as you wish.'

'Ooh, someone's got a boyfriend,' I heard the boyfriend say on Skype, as they both continued to giggle and make sweet plans for their beautiful future together.

I felt too sick to think about my future; I had no idea what the hell to expect. I just hoped Bobby wouldn't kill me. After all, I had promised my sister not to die.

I went to live in Crystal Palace on the first week of August. The sun was shining every day and the concrete walls made the city even hotter. London in August was so different from what it had been in June – both the weather and my life – that it felt almost surreal. Rain had stopped, the clouds were gone, to be replaced by the burning sun.

I had burned my bridges with everything I had known, and now I had to get busy building new ones. I was still thinking about my boy back in the hostel in Tallinn, and had imagined him holding me every night when I'd gone through another hard day. In reality, I'd never had him hold me in the first place, even when things were good.

So, what did I have left? Absolutely nothing.

5

~

Bobby was living in a three-storey building right off the high street. The house was full of mostly Jamaicans, who were smoking ganja and listening to reggae every day in front of the main door and its stairs, watching the passers-by and enjoying the weather. As a result, the doors were always open and the hallway filled with the sweet, rustic aroma of weed.

Bobby's flat was on the top floor, so it was the quietest. It was a three-bedroom flat with a big lounge, kitchen, and a bathroom. Weirdly, the place was the complete opposite of the man living there. While Bobby looked very organised, clean, and always on top of business, his place looked like it was under renovation that was never going to end. All the walls were painted white, and splashes of the work were all around the floors. The flat had very little furniture, and the few pieces that there were looked slightly broken, dirty, or forgotten under piles of books and/or clothes.

I was given the smallest room of the flat. It was so tiny it could only fit a double bed and an old, wobbly shelf, but that was enough for me. All I had with me was my small backpack and a guitar that was constantly out of tune.

My room was next to the kitchen, which had a big table, lots of chairs, a fridge, a shelf with heaps of books (mostly about Africa, Jah, music, and French), a radio, and plenty of CDs from the Marley family musicians. And brown bananas. These brown bananas were everywhere and, frankly,

I couldn't believe that a man with so much wisdom and cleanliness would have rotting fruit in his kitchen and not even blink an eye about it.

There was no warm water anywhere, but we had a kettle that became a true lifesaver. He also introduced me to the electricity stick – this was a little blue stick that we topped up at the off-licence and then plugged into the cable box so we could have electricity. I didn't even know this was possible. But this man showed me a lot of things I never knew.

Bobby treated me very well. In the mornings, after a quick breakfast, he would take his guitar and busk in Westminster station until about 6pm. I would usually spend the day sending CVs, trying to find work, while listening to Stephen Marley. In the evenings, he would come home and cook some amazing African meal for the two of us.

He introduced me to plantains (turned out they weren't rotten bananas at all, but a proper African banana type of fruit) and yams (the potato-loving Estonian in me was screaming for joy), spices, and different fiery flavours from West Africa that I had never tasted nor heard of as a North-Eastern European. He would tell me stories about Africa's history, the white Western power, the wars, the life in Ivory Coast. He told me about ISIS before they started popping up everywhere. Enthusiastically, he would tell me about his eternal love for Bob Marley and reggae music, all the while showing me pictures of himself in Marley's home in Jamaica.

Every day would be like this. He would ask me about my work search and make sure I was on it, and say, 'Jah will help anyone who will give thyself a chance.'

It seemed like Bobby liked to help out others in need as much as he could. He gave me a home at a time when I was really at the bottom, and sometimes, knowing how poor I was, he'd leave me a bit of money to buy food for the day. And lottery tickets. Oh man, did he love to play lottery! A lot of the times he let me choose the numbers without understanding how unlucky I am. He only won when I hadn't chosen the numbers.

I also met his buddy, Joe. He would come to the flat three or four times a week, watch TV, smoke a few big ones, and eat chocolate. At first, I thought he was maybe a builder (cause he always dressed like one) doing some work on the house and taking a break at ours, until he told me that he came to Bobby's to get away from his wife. Three or four times a week he'd put on these clothes, kiss his wife goodbye, and go to 'work' – aka come to his friend's to watch TV and smoke for five hours.

I didn't mind Joe. He was very nice and chilled, and he always came with a bag of chocolates that he didn't mind sharing, which was nice. Although I do wonder what his wife must have been like that he had to get away from her so often.

A few days after moving into Crystal Palace, the London riots started. The whole city was literally on fire. After seeing how people were burning buses, Bobby didn't go busking for two days. This showed me something was really wrong – this was a man who went busking even when he was half dead from fever, or it was raining cats and dogs outside.

Bobby was very careful and protective, and he decided that nobody should leave the house, which was fine by me. I didn't have enough money to do anything out there anyway. Instead, we spent those two days at home watching the news with Joe, who despite the burning city, still preferred to escape from his wife and spend time with us.

Lewisham, which had been my first home in London, was one of the main looting areas. Weirdly enough, it almost felt like seeing my childhood memories being destroyed in front of me. My mother, who thought I was still living in Lewisham, gave me a desperate call to make sure I was alright. When she heard I lived near Brixton instead, she calmed down and didn't ask any additional questions – like a true, quiet Estonian.

For the next few days, we would only go out to buy groceries, but even the shops were closed. It would be 4pm and the streets would be empty, shops closed, nobody around. The only place we could get food from was this off-licence on the corner. Even they had put a metal curtain in front of their door, and were handing goods through the hole in the wall.

I was baffled. I had only seen this kind of living in the old USSR video tapes, or heard about it through the nightmare stories my mother sometimes loved to tell about the horrendous 'Russian time', as we called it. On those videos, you could see how people queued up to get any sort of food, clothes, anything at all – at that time, everything was in short supply. The streets looked evil and apocalyptic. My mother had grown up like this, my grandmother had grown up like this. Now, here was I, their daughter and granddaughter – a 21st century girl in a big city – living it, too.

Soon enough, the looters arrived in Brixton. I remember taking a bus through Brixton to go find a job, and seeing all the shop windows boarded up with planks of wood. It literally looked like an empty, dead city. It didn't take my mom long to call me again.

'Hello,' she said in a quiet, yet indifferent tone. Translated from Estonian into real feelings, means 'I'm really worried about you'. I told her not to fear because Lemmi would take care of me and that calmed her down. Again, no additional questions were ever asked.

To this day, I've never told her that by the time those riots happened, Lemmi was already happily back in Estonia, and I was living in an abandoned house with a stranger I had just met. I've never dared to tell her. I knew she wouldn't have understood and I couldn't bear to listen to all her doubts and worries – and there would have been plenty.

I had to be strong and focus only on the good things. I was by myself now.

When I moved into Crystal Palace, Bobby had made it very clear that if I wanted to stay there I had to find a job and be productive. He couldn't stand laziness nor procrastination, and always spoke down about the Jamaicans living in the building. In his opinion, they did nothing but smoke their lives away. The friendly sweetness he showed towards me would turn into scary hostility the moment anybody mentioned the neighbours.

To avoid being on his bad side, I spent most of my days looking for a job. Every day I would apply to about 30-40 jobs online. And as soon as the riots were over, I would go out every morning with my CVs and pop them into anywhere that was hiring or looked a nice enough place to work. It was only when I had walked around aimlessly for hours and given my best fake smile (the one that wouldn't show my desperation or depression) that I'd go home, play guitar to calm my nerves, and tell Bobby, 'They might call me. They looked very promising.' Then I'd count the coins he had made busking that day, and listen to his stories as he cooked up some other great African dish.

I enjoyed spending time with him, I really did. He was wise, interesting, and very determined. But I was always scared of him, too. I needed Bobby. He was the only person I knew in London. He was the only one to give me shelter and offer me proper food, so I depended on him in every way. And he knew it. I was playing in his field with his rules; all that was needed was one wrong move and my game would have been finished.

It had been two weeks since I had moved into the place, yet hadn't managed to get a job. Two weeks too long. I could see the usual 'They might call me. They looked promising' trick wasn't working on Bobby. The secret ingredient to his food wasn't love any more, it was frustration. I could taste its bitter, disappointing flavour on my tongue, swirling in my mouth, not wanting to go down.

'I am applying to all the jobs, and I don't know why nobody wants me,' I told him once when he was stoned enough to not get angry.

'Apply better,' was his answer. Even though he said it with a smile, the words stabbed just as hard. In a way, I knew he was right. Work smart not hard. Quality before quantity. Learn to apply better, learn to sell yourself better.

I tried all the tricks under the sun. I smiled, I was attentive, I listened, I did what I was told, but all the responses were cold and indifferent – if anybody even bothered to reply. For some reason, nobody wanted to hire me even for the easiest jobs. It wasn't because of my lack of job experience in England, so it must have been something else. I just couldn't figure out what it was.

After three weeks of still no job, I could feel the tension rising in the house. In order to avoid conflict, I'd stay out as long as possible to save me from going home and talking about another failed day with Bobby. I thought, *If he can't see me, he can't be mad at me, right? I could lie to him later that I was on a trial day and perhaps he'd be nice to me.*

After selling myself for hours to potential employers, I'd go on the tube and travel aimlessly, staring at the people. I almost felt jealous when I saw people in their work clothes. They had some place to be, they were making money, they had a reason to be tired. I'd take one train after another just to kill time until 9pm when I knew Bobby would be too high to ask me serious questions.

I became good friends with his buddy, Joe, and he would help me with my job search. He taught me how to lie better on my CV and let me know about any vacancies he had seen on his way over. He was a really good guy to me, so it always remained a mystery why he lied and ran away from his wife.

A week later, I got a job through Gumtree. It seemed as though at least somebody somewhere was checking all the mail I had been sending out in the last months, and had finally decided to answer. The job was for a charity, and I had to be out on the streets selling stuff and bothering people who wanted to do everything but talk to me. Frankly, I didn't want to talk to them either. I am Estonian, after all – if I could, I would never speak to another person ever again. I also have zero selling skills – I couldn't sell myself even if my life depended on it. But hey, a girl needs to eat, and the £8 an hour I got for it felt like the most money I had ever seen. Also, in order to keep a roof over my head, I had to show Bobby I was more than just trying to be good; I actually had to be good, too.

The charity I was working for was for the training of guide dogs. I became the most hated person on the street; the one that shows up and starts talking to you with the biggest smile. I hate these people myself, but now, I was one of them. It was my job to get people to sign up and give £4 a month so that guide dogs could be trained and then given to help the blind or other disabled people.

Yes, I hated being on the streets. And yes, I hated approaching people and forcing them to listen to sad stories of puppies and the disabled, when I could see all they wanted to do was get on with their day. It's certainly not my favourite thing to do.

Nevertheless, it was a noble job and I knew my discomfort was for a good cause. Funnily enough, this important and necessary charity that helps people in need in a massively great way, gets very little funding from the government. The only way they keep on going is due to the donations from the people (on the streets and online) and the volunteers that work for them.

The most successful workers there were all aspiring actors or other performers. They managed to stay upbeat, enthusiastic, and cheerful all day long, whereas the others, including me, were barely standing up by the end of the day. Why? Because the amount of angry NO's you hear per minute, the judgemental looks you get along with them, and the overall feeling that you're the black plague, are all really soul-destroying. It takes a lot of acting to stay driven and upbeat in that job. People will do anything – and I mean ANYTHING – to get out of talking to you. Sometimes it was even quite funny.

I am a bad actress and, as I mentioned before, an even worse salesperson, so I didn't do very well. After some time, I started approaching people just to hear what their angry voice sounded like. *This guy looks fit, will he tell me to fuck off softly or will he pout disapprovingly? This older woman, will she send me to hell in a sweet motherly voice, or will she hit me with her dog and curse me to the ground instantly?* You never knew what reaction you would get.

It became like a videogame to me. I was Super Mario and my mission was to catch as many stars (people saying 'no') as possible. I got so into the game that, honestly, when somebody did say yes and agreed to talk to me about the cause, I didn't even know what to say any more. It's like you're so used to being defeated that when you finally have a chance to win, it feels so unbelievable you mess it up on purpose.

Even though the job was hard, the people working there were great. We even went dancing one night, and they started calling me 'The Nordic princess' – although, Lord knows, I resembled more of a prince. It was also the first place that asked me for a NANO, explained to me what it was, and taught me how to get one.

My mission to help blind people and their dogs came to an end quite abruptly, after just two weeks of working there. One morning, as I was about to go to work, it turned out I didn't have enough money on my Oyster nor on any of my bank cards to buy a train ticket. I didn't even have £4 to get to work to make money! I ran back home, hoping to find some coins lying around, but no luck. Bobby had already left, otherwise he could have helped me out. Payday was only three days away and I had to survive these days somehow.

I called work to tell them about my situation and to apologise for being late / not showing up, and said I'd make sure to be there first thing Monday. The guy on the other end said, 'Don't worry. Thank you for your services.'

I didn't know what that was supposed to mean and I didn't have a chance to ask, because he hung up. No letters sent; no calls answered.

My P45 arrived along with my final pay check a few days later, after the weekend. Great. Another place that was happy to let me go. Four fucking pounds! I'd managed to get quite a few people to sign up to give £4 a month to this charity, and we always used to say, '£4 is not a lot; it´s a small amount for a big cause!' Yet I lost my job because I didn't have that damn £4 to give. Where are the charities when you need them most?

I didn't dare to tell Bobby I was jobless again. I just couldn't bear to see his disappointed face, and I couldn't risk being kicked out. It was a thought that was constantly playing in the back of my head.

I had nowhere to go and barely any money. The pay from the charity for my 10 working days was quickly spent on train tickets and food. For the next two weeks, I kept up my little game of waking up early in the morning, having a quick bite, then heading off to 'work'. Actually, I would go walking around Crystal Palace park for a few hours until I knew he'd be out, then I could return home to apply for jobs online, hoping to get something before he could catch out my lie.

There were about 15 people living in the building, most of them Jamaicans, and all of them spending their days smoking on the outside stairs. I got along with everybody in the house, and I even became good friends with the Indian guys in our local off-licence. But one guy, who hated my guts and made sure I knew it, was the leader of the gang, the biggest Rastafarian, the main man of our building. Every time I would come in or out and greet the neighbours, he would stay quiet and look me up and down, his eyes judging my whole existence and purpose in this life. The moment I passed him, I could hear him kiss his teeth and ask others, loudly enough for me to hear, 'What is this whitey doing here? Who is she? Fucking white trash!'

His words were full of hate and his tone vicious, like he was ready to battle with this 'whitey' right there. Even though the others told him to calm down and not to worry about it, he'd still mouth off that it was 'his house'. This was a 'black house'. My 'pale ass and different accent' was not welcomed here. The words 'whitey' and 'white fucking trash' had echoed in this house's stone hallways every day since I had started living there, but become louder and harsher in time.

This went on for weeks and weeks, and got worse after I lost the charity job and was unemployed again. Then I had to listen to him all day long, asking others if this 'whitey' was still living here, then kissed his teeth and angrily rolled another cigarette when the others said I did.

I never said anything. I greeted his first judgemental looks with a smile, hoping he would see my good side and ease up. But not giving into his provocations made him even meaner, to the point that I avoided going out when he was at the front, because I knew he might get physical. When I opened the windows, I would hear all the things he'd like to do to the 'white trash living upstairs', so I kept them closed despite the hot September days.

What was I supposed to say to him anyway? What *CAN* you say to something like that? I understand you don't have to like everybody you meet, but to judge somebody based on their appearance is a cheap shot and just shows the bully's own ignorance. I can't all of a sudden change my colour – I'm not a chameleon – nor would I want to. Fucking hell. I had always thought that big multi-cultural countries like the UK, the USA, etc, would be used to diversity, so racism would be an ancient and non-existent problem. How wrong I was. How silly. Racism is alive and unfortunately happening all the time, especially in places that you'd think would already be used to all the differences.

Bobby and I would have long discussions about race. As a black man, he would have to defend himself at least once a day to random people that liked to remark about his colour.

Fortunately for me, Mr. Big Man got taken away one evening by the police. It seemed that I wasn't the only person the man hated; one day when they decided to change their usual joints for Special K ciders, he bottled his friend on the head. The friend got taken away on a stretcher and Mr. Big Man got taken away by the police for a couple of days.

He was a changed man when he came back. He kept more to himself and didn't call me names any more. From that night on, he barely even looked at me.

Even though the hallway reeked of old blood, artificial cleaning, and dirty water weeks after the incident, I was happy to be able to move freely without a constant reminder that I was a 'white trash whitey'. When the Big Man was gone, the other neighbours started talking to me, and I would even spend some time chatting to them outside, whereas before I had just passed them politely as quickly as possible.

Our conversations weren't too long, because their strong Jamaican accents were very hard for me to understand. Their every other sentence to me was, 'Do you know what I'm sayin'?' Trying not to look like an idiot who didn't speak English, I'd say that I did. I tried to understand them, I really did. And sometimes I did, but most of the time not really. One time, I mentioned my low English language skills to Bobby.

'Nobody understands them, they're Jamaicans. Only they understand each other's strong accents, that's why they stick together,' was his answer. 'Anyways, you shouldn't talk to them. They have no life. You need to work and stay away from them.'

Yeah. I knew they weren't gonna be my friends – I could barely understand them – but I had spent over a month being basically by myself and had nobody to talk to, so I grabbed onto every opportunity to have any sort of interaction. It didn't matter if they were deaf or mute, or even if they spoke an accent so strong I had no idea whether we were talking about bacon or beer cans. I was craving for a simple human connection so badly. I didn't know it was humanly possible to miss something like that.

People always like to ask, 'What was the hardest part of moving to another country? How did you cope with the changes? How did you find your way?'

You see, Estonia and England are actually very similar countries, despite being on different sides of Europe. We are both stuck with shitty weather – both of our winters last for eight months and summers for eight days. Due to our *beautiful* weather, we are all pale and tired human beings. In order to get through the day, we amuse ourselves with dark, sarcastic humour over a beer… or five. And we all speak English with minor mistakes. Even my grandmother who grew up in the USSR-time can speak a few sentences and understands simple things. The number of mistakes, especially when writing, that English people make in their own mother tongue is outstanding and unbelievable. So, we're almost on the same page here.

Of course, there are differences when it comes to the size and the daily lifestyle of the countries, but overall I found there was nothing shocking or unusual to see or learn. So, what was the hardest part of moving to a new country? What were the biggest obstacles for me?

Loneliness.

Frankly, I never believed how much a human could miss others. I had always been an introvert, loved being by myself, and had wandered off into my own world even when I was surrounded by people. But after spending almost four months in London, where I had no personal human contact besides weird job trials and racist comments, I started to feel that every cell in my body longed, craved, pleaded for a simple human touch, even if it was just a superficial hug or a cold handshake. I never knew this could happen to a human being.

And with loneliness came depression.

That damn, silent bitch that creeps up on you in your darkest hour and paralyses your whole body, plays with your mind, and lowers your emotions to the point that you feel like your own shadow has more consistency and worth than you.

I had felt like just half a person since the day I moved to London in June, and three months later – early September – it was just as bad. Before I'd had Lemmi to lean on, because she felt the same way. Now, I had nobody. I couldn't talk to Bobby about any of my emotions or fears. Honestly, I didn't even know how to verbalize the void I carried in me.

I also knew he couldn't stand any sort of excuses or giving up. That's why I had been so happy working for the charity. Being surrounded by young, upbeat people made me forget my own troubles, and gave me hope to keep going. When I lost that job, I also lost all the connection to these people, as well as my reason to get up in the morning. The only people I knew in London were the Jamaicans at the front door, the Indians in the off-licence, and Bobby. But none of them was really my friend.

I remember looking out of the big windows in the lounge on those warm August and September evenings. The sun would settle behind the Shard, Gherkin, and Canary Wharf's tall buildings. Enviously, I would stare at people walking on the high street, joking with their friends at the bus stop, going in and out of pubs. Couples. Friends. Families. Everybody had somebody, everybody was laughing and enjoying the summer evenings. In Estonia, I had been like that, too. In Estonia, I used to have friends. I used to laugh. As I was staring at those happy people, I couldn't even remember the last time I had slightly smirked.

I used to hop onto crowded buses and enjoy the rush hours when tube carriages were crammed with people. These were the only moments when I had any sort of human contact, when I could feel my numb body melting and slowly becoming human again. We were all forced to stand with our backs against each other, unintentional hand touches, breathing the same stale air, stepping on each other's feet... My usual nightmare used to be my sweetest dream.

It felt so beautiful that sometimes I'd close my eyes and let myself feel every bump, touch, and squeeze that the frustrated people give each other on crammed trains. They probably thought that I was tired from working all day and that I was sleeping standing up. Actually, I was just happy to be part of civilization, part of the human race, and I absorbed every second and touch that I could.

I know it sounds weird. If I saw somebody on the train being sexually aroused from me stepping on their foot and elbowing them in the face, I'd change carriage and tell them to get help. As a matter of fact, I would have liked it if somebody had just talked to me – even if it was about my mental health, or just yelling at my weirdness. But nobody did.

To avoid going crazy and to show Bobby I was busy working/getting a job, I would take long walks in the parks and wander around Regent Street looking for work. There were always people who were either out with their dogs playing ball, or curious tourists looking in awe at the buildings. As much as the sight of other happy people reminded me of my own sadness, in the few moments when our eyes would meet and I could play with their dog, I felt energised, I felt noticed. At that time, a stranger's smile or a beautiful word meant everything to me. It truly did.

Let me tell you how I found out that chips in England are called 'crisps' and fries are 'chips'. All of my English slang and language skills had come from American music, TV shows, and films. So, one afternoon when I walked out of Sainsbury's with a small bag of crisps, I found these youngsters making music in the corner of the shop. They were having fun, coming up with beats and playing guitar, and I was instantly drawn to them. *Perhaps I could play my white trash out-of-tune guitar to them and we could jam together? Maybe they could become my first friends in England?* Music really does get people together.

I approached them, enjoying the beats and the happy people. Watching them and enjoying their creativity made me feel like I was in the happy music videos I had watched as a kid. Things were looking up.

When I locked eyes with this guy who was rapping some rhymes and smiling at me, I offered him some chips. The music stopped.

'Chips? You call THESE CHIPS?! OY, can y'all hear it what she said – chips!' The whole crowd started laughing. 'These are not chips, these are crisps!'

This was the last time in my damn life I called potato crisps 'chips', I swear. Nobody wanted my food, and nobody wanted to talk to me, see me, be with me. They laughed at my language incompetence loudly and for a long time, then continued playing music as if I wasn't there. So I left.

I ate the crisps by myself at the park, while choking on their words and laughter. I was so sick of Crystal Palace park that even though the place is gorgeous, I couldn't set my foot in it, even if I got paid for it. Every tree, every corner of this wonderful park, reminds me of the hollow loneliness I suffered from while I walked there for hours, trying to find some sort of sense to my life in that summer and early autumn.

6

~

I had been living in Crystal Palace for just over a month-and-a-half when things started to get very weird, and I realised I had to get out fast. It all started with Bobby leaving for a week to go to France.

On my usual depressed kind of day, I met a guy waiting in front of our house. He was young, good-looking, and spoke English without a Jamaican accent, so I was surprised he was there. It turned out he was a cousin of one of the guys living in the building.

We talked for a long time, me hanging on his every word and breath, because he was young and he was nice to me. Everything was fine until he asked me about Michel.

'How is your relationship with Michel going? All good?'

I told him he must have mistaken me for somebody else; I didn't know any Michel, I wasn't in a relationship with anybody, and I was living with Bobby.

He started laughing. 'Bobby?! Ha, ha, haa!' He was laughing louder than the traffic on the high street. He almost clapped his hands, that's how funny this whole situation was for him.

'Alright, alright, Bobby then! So, if you two ain't in a relationship, why is he saying that you are? He's been telling everyone in the building that's why you're living together, that you guys are in love! And now you say you don't even know his name? Ha, ha, ha!'

Oh my, was he having fun. He wouldn't stop laughing. He had just found his pot of gold and couldn't hide his excitement. The fact that I didn't know any of the things that were supposedly going on in my life was hilarious for him.

'Oh man, this is funny. Creepy, too, though... I don't know,' he added when he saw I wasn't laughing. Before I could ask him any questions, his cousin came out and they left.

I didn't know what to say. I can't say I was surprised. I had known from the very beginning that Bobby had a hidden agenda when inviting me to his place, but I had decided to turn a blind eye to it because I had nowhere else to go. There were texts during daytime to which I never replied, and after he had smoked a few in the evenings, he always liked to know what the future might bring for me, for us. My usual answer was 'I don't know, I'm tired', then I'd go to my room, lock the door, and pretend to sleep just to avoid whatever further talking could bring.

Usually, Bobby kept all the papers, documents, mail, and pictures away, and took care of everything himself. I never questioned his slightly controlling ways, because I felt like it was none of my business to go through somebody else's things. The man had lived there for six years, so who knew what was in his mailbox? But I was waiting for my NANO to arrive, and since Bobby was away, I kept a very close eye on the mail.

That's when I realised – everything was addressed to Michel. Bobby only existed between me and him, in the upper flat, nowhere else. In an instant, I understood all the surprising faces and silly laughs I had always received from the neighbours when I mentioned his name. I also found some pictures of him and his ex-lover. The woman in the photo looked exactly as I had looked on the day we met in Westminster – white, blonde, curly hair, small flowy top, a little make-up.

Bobby had mentioned his relationship before and had said that the woman looked similar to me, but this picture was almost like looking at myself. No wonder when he approached me in the station, he'd spoken to me like I was his old friend. He probably mistook me for his ex, and later it had been too awkward to back off.

And his name – Bobby? The man sang Bob Marley. Of course his name was going to be Bobby. It all made sense now.

I felt like a character in an Agatha Christie crime novel, putting together the pieces for a murder yet to be committed. Like all the English thrillers my mom loves to watch, her daughter was living in one herself. In England. If only my mother knew.

I knew I had to get out before Bobby… sorry, Michel… came home, but I just didn't know where to go. I had about three days to come up with a new plan and make it work for me. The next day, Joe came around and I asked him about Michel. He just laughed. I never saw him again.

I went to the only other people I knew in this town – the Jamaicans – and asked if they knew any other places, any squats, anything at all. Frankly, they were too stoned to even talk, and the few words they did mutter were complete gibberish, even to each other. The best 'advice' I got was from an English girl called Tammy. Besides me, she was the only whitey in the block, and didn't have a Jamaican accent. She was loud and strong like the boys, yet the few times I saw her hanging out on the stairs, she was also very sweet.

Hearing about my problem, she told me to go to the council and get a free flat. She had always bragged about living in her own place and was happy that she didn't have to live in a squat, like we did.

'It's your right, babe, they have to give it to ya,' she'd say. 'When you's pregnant, they have to provide a liveable space for ya, innit. Cause you's getting a baby, innit, they can't just leave ya on the streets, d'ya know what I mean? Go to the council, swear down, it's your right, babe.'

It turned out she had gotten knocked up by one of the guys in our building and had another one on the way (as she proudly declared while smoking away), and that's why she had the flat. She insisted I do the same. It was my right, after all, and I should grab onto it. Because, fuck the government, right?

I felt disgusted. Getting knocked up just so I could have a flat? That was definitely not the way I planned on living my life. I felt trapped and for the first time in my life, I was actually scared. By finding out his real identity, I had made a fatal mistake in Bobby's game and I had got on the bad side of this man. I knew it was time for me to go.

Two more days until Bobby's (or Michel's?) return.

I started Googling squats and found out there was a meeting held for squatters every second Wednesday – to meet up, share information, and get help. The next one was in a week. So, I just had to survive for seven days without getting knocked up, killed, or even something worse.

A few days later, Bobby arrived home with a note from the council saying everybody had to attend court and would probably be evicted in the next few weeks. He was furious that I had the lights on, and said that from now on, we had to pretend as if the house was abandoned and nobody lived there any more. We had to enter and exit the building in secret, and to live as if we didn't exist.

From the evening he returned from his trip, he was always angry and frustrated. He treated me like a bad omen, because he had peacefully lived in the building for over six years and it was about to be taken away from him just when I arrived. I asked what would happen to him.

'Government has to give me a new place to live. I've been here for over six years, so they can't just put me out on the streets. If you've lived somewhere long enough, they can't just get rid of you without offering something back,' he'd say.

As I said before, the man was very organised and determined in every aspect of his life. He wasn't gonna go down without a fight, so he began collecting papers from years ago to prove his words in court.

'But you need to leave,' he told me. 'You must have some money now, you've worked for couple of weeks. You can afford to rent a place now. Do it now.' He barely even looked at me, too busy with his papers.

'Sure,' I mumbled back. He thought I still had the job that had finished three weeks before, and I still didn't have the guts to tell him that I didn't. He was already frustrated and I was afraid the truth would send him overboard. So I just nodded my head, said nothing, and prayed to angels that next Wednesday would come quicker.

From that night onwards, we didn't share any more meals or talks. I would stay in my room behind a locked door when he was home, because I was afraid of what would be said or done next. Sometimes I would hear him through the walls, cursing me while he was in the kitchen, maybe thinking I wouldn't hear him.

'Fuck her, low-life girl! Fuck her, sleeping her life away!'

The truth was, I wasn't sleeping. During those weeks, I hardly slept at all. I just stayed hidden because I was so afraid.

The only job offers I got during that time were hostessing jobs at gentlemen's clubs around Soho and Leicester Square. I thought I could handle that, but I found it hard to even stay for the interviews. As soon as I walked in, I could feel men watching me as though I was a piece of meat and they were all hungry hyenas, ready to play with me while they were slowly killing me. Their lustful eyes travelling on my body (every-thing but the face), along with the sensual music, alcohol fumes, and the dim, sexy decor of the clubs, made me want to run away as soon as I entered. I know money was tight and perhaps, for my future's sake, I should have just gone through with working there. But I felt so uncomfortable being objecti-fied like this that I simply couldn't.

That Wednesday evening was warm and pleasant. The meeting was held in a small shop-like building that slightly reminded me of the booze kiosks I'd seen in my childhood. On its walls were heaps of cut-out newspaper articles regard-ing politics, empty houses, law changes, squats, posters about squatting rules and rights. They were offering free tea and bis-cuits, but I had never been big on hot drinks and was too nervous to talk, so I just stood there awkwardly.

Fortunately, a young English guy started talking to me. Other youngsters nearby heard us and a group of eight was quickly formed. Our little crew was full of young students and workers who, due to high rent prices and low or non-existent wages, had been forced to turn to squatting. None of us had ever done that before. I know had been squatting for the last two months, but what was about to come was a completely different experience.

Of the eight of us, the only two people without any responsibilities (no work, no school) were me and this sunny hipster boy, Austin from Seattle, who I had already noticed at the meeting. We decided to meet up the next day and form a plan for the whole crew, choosing Camden to be the most like-able area for us to live in.

I got back home late at night, careful not to wake Bobby/Michel. From that moment on, I tried to be as invisible to him as possible.

Austin was a 23-year-old from Seattle who had just arrived in London, and was planning to spend the next seven months travelling around Europe. He had decided to start in London – the home of his idols, David Bowie, The Rolling Stones, The Kinks, The Clash, T-Rex… well, basically every punk/rock icon of the 60s and 70s.

He dressed like an androgynous cowboy (minus the straw hat and a horse) and looked like a mixture of Hugh Grant, David Bowie, and Clint Eastwood. His accent was a mixture of American Disneyland blended together with old English phrases that his idols used to say. When he was nervous, he sounded like Mickey Mouse on helium.

The next few days were spent mostly wandering around Camden and Mornington Crescent, looking at houses and wondering if any of them were empty. But to be honest, neither of us really knew anything about squatting, and it isn't something that anybody can just randomly start doing. You need to know the law, have patience and a good eye, if you want to be serious about it. Hence all the articles and posters about rights and rules in the squatters' meeting.

At that time, of course, neither of us knew anything about it. Austin had just arrived in England and was living in a hostel, and although I'd lived at Bobby's for two months, I'd never encountered any squatting rules before. Bobby's place had all been sorted out by the time I got there, and all I had to do was keep quiet about it. The only rules I'd had to follow were Bobby's own, but I had disobeyed even them.

So Austin and I would wander around day after day, only to be met by beautiful buildings that were definitely not empty.

Also, we didn't even have much to talk about. I found his brown, silky, 70s shirt and beret a ridiculous combination, and he found my black sandals with huge shiny flowers just as bad. Bobby (Michel) had brought them to me from France when he saw I had been wearing the same winter boots for the whole of summer. 'I know what women like to wear, I know their taste,' he'd said proudly, and I'd thanked him out of politeness. They looked hideous, but I simply couldn't wear my old broken boots any longer.

After walking around aimlessly for hours, we decided to sit down by the docks and have a beer to lighten our mood.

'Interesting shoes,' Austin said, pointing at the huge flowers on top of the toes of my sandals. He took a huge sip of his beer, probably to forget the ugly image he had just seen.

'They are fucking awful, that's what they are. But I have nothing else to wear.' I had a sip of my beer to do the same.

He started laughing, breaking the ice between us. 'That's what I actually meant to say.'

We started to meet every day, looking for potential squats for our crew but also to drink beer and soak up the sweet autumn sun while we talked about everything and nothing at all. We became very good friends and I was so happy that I had finally met someone who took away the loneliness of my days and replaced it with adventure and the fun of being young and free. We were just two kids away from home, ready to take on whatever the future had in hold for us.

Austin had obviously done a better job at the squatters' meeting than me and made some pretty good contacts with people who actually knew about this lifestyle. He kept in touch with a guy called Tom, who said he knew about a place in Finchley Road.

Tom reckoned our new crew would be the perfect guinea pigs to test out this little cottage he had found. It was right by the high street and, according to him, nobody had been in there for weeks, maybe even months. It seemed perfect for squatting, although we would still have to be cautious.

For us, this was perfect. Bobby had become particularly anxious and hesitant about me being in the house, and the nice texts he'd sent me when we first met had been replaced with 'Do you have a new place already? You must get out, quickly!'

Austin was also tired of living in a hostel and sharing a room with ten other snoring, stinking fellas. So, this information about a possible new home felt like God's gift.

7

~

We met up on a Thursday evening at the station when it had already started to get dark. Tom, Austin, me, and Herbert – one of the German guys from our first night – were supposed to be the guinea pigs for the night to test the house. I had told Bobby the day before that I had found a place, but had lied that I was renting a place with all the money I had gained from the supposed job I'd had for months now. His answer was a simple careless shrug and 'Great, you can go now'.

In the evening, I packed my two bags and guitar, and left the keys on the kitchen table. Bobby still hadn't returned from busking. These days, he too was staying out longer and later, doing God knows what. It wasn't my business any more; it had never been my business in the first place. But from being two friends (sort of) at the beginning, we were now stranger than strangers. I was certain that I wasn't going to come back to Crystal Palace any more and would probably never see Bobby again.

As a final farewell, I wrote him a letter which I left on the kitchen table along with the keys.

Dear Bobby,

Thank you for everything. You gave me a home at a time when I really needed it.

I wish you all the best. Good luck at the court!

PS: Also say bye to Joe for me.

Thanks, bye! Eva

I never heard from Bobby again, and I doubt he ever forwarded my greetings to Joe. I hadn't seen the man in over a week, and wondered if he had accepted his faith with the wife or found a new place to run away from her.

The four of us met by the station, along with our few bags of clothes. Three of us were as excited as young puppies off to new adventures, while Tom was quiet, calm, and cautious. Even in the evening darkness, I could feel his brown eyes examining each of us thoroughly. He then took us to the little house that looked like a small, cosy cottage in the middle of the city.

We got in through a little crack in the side door. The first thing I could smell was a flowery, warm air – the kind you usually smell at grandmothers' places and that makes you instantly feel like at home. I hadn't smelt anything other than mould, sweat, and a cold breeze in the last few months, so I was immediately filled with joy as we wandered inside.

Tom was in front, leading the way, then Austin, me, and Herbert doing exactly what our leader said. We found ourselves in a big lounge, with a king-sized bed (my favourites from the cleaning times), a fireplace, a few bookshelves, and warm, dark blue carpet on the floors. The place was gorgeous.

Tom immediately went to see the other rooms and we were right behind him. Besides the lounge and the kitchen, all the other rooms were unfurnished and dirty, as if somebody had left the place in a rush, having run away from something. We checked the rooms quietly, careful not to touch or break anything.

After going through every room and not finding a single soul or any sign of anybody, we sat down and caught our breaths. Although the place was warm and cosy, it still felt like anybody could come in at any minute and kick us out. We were in somebody else's property, after all.

It was dark, but Tom encouraged us to only use candles for lighting. From his bag, he took out a box of matches and a few candles, and placed them around the lounge so that we could finally see the room more clearly. In the dim light, Tom's calm presence reminded me of Buddha; the rest of us had excited red faces and huge curious eyes as we examined our surroundings, all new to this whole situation.

Tom sat us all around in a circle and asked how we were. 'Great!' we all answered with a childish, yet slightly scared excitement. We had no idea what we had just done and what we were going to do. Understanding our ignorance, Tom took out a paper called Section 75 from his bag and put it up on the front door. He then taught us the Squatting 101.

1. Squatting is not trespassing. You only enter the buildings that you have kept your eye on for a while and have made sure are abandoned. Do not ever break your way in – this would be called vandalising, which is criminally punishable. Seek and you shall find; you'd be surprised how almost every house has an open door, window, or crack somewhere, that lets you in easily. But never break your way in, ever.

2. Once in and sure that the place is available, put up Section 75 on a clear, obvious place (usually the front door). Section 75 is part of the Criminal Justice and Public Order Act (1994) that states on discovery of an unlawful occupant, the owner of the premises has to give the occupiers 48 hours notice before going to the police and/or court. Overall, it is a very civil, peaceful paper (and a law), which, unfortunately, the other part never really adhered to.

3. It's always better to squat with a group. It is safer, more secure, and more fun. If shit goes down, you always need a back-up.

4. When inside, try to find out who the place belongs to. There must be some letters or notes with somebody's name on it. Try to inform them that you're squatting at their place peacefully, and hopefully you can reach an agreement that would suit both of you. There are plenty of squats in London alone where the occupants and owners have a good deal going on.

5. The most important rule of all – know the law. Know your rights as a squatter and their rights as the building owners. Know the address of the place you are squatting, both post-code and street name. Squatting is not just a carousel ride. You might not pay rent, but you have to pay shitloads of attention to what is constantly happening around you, so stay informed at all times. Keep in touch with other squatters so you can help each other when needed (and everybody will have a time when they do need assistance). Knowing the law determines how long and if you can squat at all.

We listened to him in awe like little children listen to their teacher on the first day at school, slightly scared but curious, trying to take everything in.

'Do you all understand?' Tom asked. We did. Sort of.

Then he took bread, ham, and cream cheese out of his bag. It was a small rucksack that seemed to store an endless supply of all sorts of goodies.

'Now, let's eat. Soon I'm gonna show you the best skips where you can always find some fresh bread and other groceries. It's a funny life, you know. People throw away perfectly good food, whereas half of the world is starving, and they leave places like this abandoned, whereas the homelessness only keeps growing."

We ate the sandwiches all in one go and talked more about the unfairness of life and squatting in general. Once the candles died out, we fell asleep. I didn't sleep well that night and kept waking up. Every time I dozed off, I dreamt of angry Bobby invading our new, flowery-smelling cottage with the police. The rules of the new life I was about to start living kept playing through my mind with all sorts of scenarios, both good and bad, like a blinking flashlight.

Our Section 75 was placed on the outside door, informing people that we were there, but in all honesty, if anybody had come in that night, I would have probably died. I was already anxious, scared, and unsure if I could follow the rules and live this life. But what other choice did I have? I had no money to buy a nice meal, far less rent a place. And because of that, I had to shut up, act brave, and keep on going.

Wasn't this what I had always dreamt of – living abroad, meeting cool people? Yes. Shut up then.

Over the next few days, all our group was living together. The house had two floors, but out of respect for the owner and for our own safety, we all stayed in the one big living room on the first floor. We all took turns who got to sleep on the bed (three at a time, so everything would be fair), while the others spent their night on the floor with their sleeping bags, spread across the two rooms.

Tom also taught us about 'skipping'. The first few days he stayed with us, our long kitchen table was full of sweets, bread, biscuits, and sometimes cheese and ham that he had brought from the skips. This was unreal. We had literally kilos of food that had been thrown out by the supermarkets, yet it tasted just as fresh and tasty as when bought. I had never seen this much food in my life before; even my family's Christmas table couldn't compare to what we had there. It was unreal. We all spent half of our days in a sugar coma, yet the mountain of sweets on the table was still not shrinking.

Oh, did I mention the best thing about this place? It. Had. A. Working. Shower.

Oh my God. Oh my dear Lord. In the last two-and-a-half months I'd only felt freezing cold or boiling water on my hands and body. Washing my hair had meant suffering from a strong headache for half a day because the water was so cold. Washing bits of my body had been more like a sprinkling water game, as it was always either freezing or boiling. But I had never felt like I had the right to complain or ask questions, because at least I had a roof over my head.

Actually, I had become used to not washing myself at all. Funnily enough, your body starts cleaning itself after some time. Kings and queens seldom washed themselves, too, and I was in Royal England, after all. If I had arrived four centuries before, I'm sure I would have fitted right in. But in 2011, I liked to keep that fun fact to myself.

My first shower in months was one of the most beautiful memories of my life. I swear. That moment, as simple as taking a shower, is still one of the purest and happiest moments of my life. It felt like the warm water was washing away all my sins and past sadness all at once. I had never understood how such a simple thing could mean so much. As ridiculous as it may seem, I was ready to give up all my dreams in order to experience it again.

I read about an experiment once where people helped to groom the homeless. They were able to take a shower, got their clothes washed and dried, and were given a haircut and a shave. After their make-over, all of them said they felt as though they could conquer the world; they felt so new, so fresh. It's funny, isn't it? It is such a simple action that everybody takes for granted without understanding what a luxury it actually is. I had taken it for granted, too. But from that night onwards, I took a shower almost twice a day, to make up for the times I'd missed out.

As they say, when it rains it pours. During the week I was settling into my new lifestyle and had given up hope of finding work, I got a job as an assistant at a fancy bag shop. I guess I had applied to it some time in the summer, and they had finally decided to contact me two months later. Within a week, my life turned from having all the time in the world to having no time at all.

I was very grateful for the job, but as I think you've already understood, selling wasn't really my strong point. I really don't know how I got the job, and I kinda felt bad for even accepting it. But still, I was making £6.50 an hour, and I now had friends, a place with a working shower, and a table full of sweets. I felt happier than ever.

We all loved living at the Finchley Road, but unfortunately, our squat didn't last for long. After two weeks of living in the cottage and working at a new place, Austin ran to my work one evening to inform me that we no longer had a home. The thought of not having a working shower made me want to cry on the spot.

It's a weird feeling talking to people and making them buy things that cost more money than you have had in your bank account in the last two months, and all the while not being sure where you'll sleep that night. 'It's a very useful bag, durable and waterproof,' I'd tell them, all the while wondering if it was durable and waterproof enough to be used as a dry spot if I had to sleep outside the following nights. I highly doubted that.

Frankly, it was time for me to get used to that feeling, because the scenario was the first of many to come. Facing an unknown future and being constantly prepared for the worst is part of the squatting lifestyle. Fortunately, everybody loved the sunny American boy, so he always managed to get us shelter.

That particular night, after the little nervous breakdown and following a few more bag sales, we moved to our new home in Greenwich.

That night, though, our little crew got torn apart and all its pieces scattered around London. Everything happened so fast and unexpectedly that nothing could be planned, so everybody had to survive in their own way. Austin and I went to Greenwich – to a place where Tom and his crew had been squatting for a few months – while others went either to their friends or had something else going on. I never saw most of them again.

Our new home was a huge glasshouse overlooking the business buildings in Canary Wharf, right by the River Thames. At one time, it had been used as a nightclub, so we had everything there except the drinks. We had a bar, tables, stools, sofas, and a dancefloor, along with the many secret rooms and big toilets. Our entrance was through the back door in the long hall, which had probably been used as a place for drunken hook-ups during the nightclub times. I have to admit, it was all pretty fancy; even the stairs were made of glass. The lights from the city lit our place enough.

There were about ten people living in this beautiful building, and they were all cheerful and welcoming when we arrived. Everybody wanted to know what had happened in Finchley Road. Sitting in a circle on the couches and barstools, surrounded by many candles and the city lights, Austin described to everyone what had happened in our lovely little flowery-smelling cottage.

He explained how he and a few of the others had woken up to loud noises coming from behind the door, and discovered there were two Russian mafiosos battering down the door with an axe, screamed at Austin in an unrecognisable language and kicked everybody's belongings out. The street and driveway were full of our clothes, books, bags, whatever anybody had brought with them, and whatever the Russians could get their hands on. Everybody grabbed what they could, even if it wasn't their own belongings. I lost a whole plastic bag full of clothes.

It was quite a funny story to listen to, and we all laughed about it that evening, but Austin was still shaken by his near-death experience. The poor fella had come to Europe only a month before, yet had already almost lost his life. He had graduated without seeing any school shootings, which is becoming a rarity in America, and hadn't been prepared for what Europe had to offer him.

One thing we never understood was why the owner had decided to kick in his own front door. We would have left the premises if he had just asked us; that's why we had always tried to contact him. I can understand that squatters have a bad reputation, and most people's first thought when they hear their property has squatters is fear – and a determination to get those 'looters' out. But that wasn't the case at all with us. We were just normal people, ready to talk. Instead, he hired the Russian Mafiosos (I'm sure they didn't do it for free), had to order a new front door (that was definitely not free), then replace all the other stuff the mafiosos broke. I heard that they enjoyed rambling round the house, breaking everything they could once they'd kicked our stuff out.

All of this could have been avoided with a little communication. But what do I know? Maybe the home owner was minted, and paying money for hitmen and his home supplies was nothing for him. Maybe he even found it entertaining. Who knows how a rich mind works? By breaking into his own house like that, he did break the law, though. Yet who cares?

When it comes to the law, the poor underdog always loses, even when he´s actually in the right.

There were about ten people already living in the glass nightclub by the time Austin and I got there on that dark October evening. Half of them were a bit older (by that I mean older than us three punks in our 20s), and the other half around our age. They had all been squatting for a long time and knew the law and politics like the back of their hands.

During the day, they were all good citizens, going to work and paying taxes; at night, they were living in abandoned buildings and eating food gathered from the bins. They were the first English people I had lived with since coming to England, and they all spoke like Sean, my dear old friend in Tallinn. No matter what you asked from them, they always had an answer. They joked, they laughed, but they remained cautious at all times. With them, I felt right at home.

During the next few weeks, we newcomers became good friends with the oldies, and we all learned a lot about the law. My days were spent in a capitalist world being slave to the wage, smiling as I sold unnecessary items to rich, careless people, while my nights were spent fighting against that same world. But I guess you have to choose your battles, and can´t fight all of them at once.

I came to understand what squatting and skipping were actually about. In the summer, when I'd met Bobby (I´ll still call him that), I had started living in his squat not out of any political movement but due to lack of money. Honestly, I had never thought about squatting being anything more than a way of punks saving money (and a way of forming bands like the Sex Pistols and the Clash). Skipping was new to me, and I was slightly hesitant about the idea, but my empty stomach could never resist a table full of sweets. And I soon came to realize it didn't make much difference where the food came from anyway.

With this new crew, I understood that we were part of something much bigger and much more serious. I had always considered the hippy-looking people eating from the bins and sleeping rough to be sad vagabonds, but now I had become one of them. And no, I wasn't sad. As a matter of fact, I felt like I was finally doing something meaningful and worthy. And I was doing it with a great bunch of people, who were happier, stronger, and smarter than all the people I met during my 'normal' daytime life.

Not all of our fellow residents were squatting because they couldn't afford to rent a place; some of them definitely could. But they wanted to draw the government's attention to an ongoing, horrible problem which this nation has: homelessness.

As the rent prices in London increase year by year, so does the number of people who are forced to live on the streets. At the same time, while people are struggling to pay £500+ a month for one small room, there are empty buildings that stand unused and uncared for. That's when squatting comes in. These people who just simply can't afford to pay hundreds each month in rent, go and live in those abandoned buildings.

People who know nothing about squatting seem to hate them and think they are freeloading looters. The truth is that during my time squatting, I never saw anybody looting or destroying the premises we were in, nor any of the other squats we visited. As a matter of fact, everybody treated the places like their own home.

And they weren't all skipping because they couldn't afford to buy a meal – again, some of them definitely could. They did it to make the government and supermarkets understand how much perfectly edible, great food they throw away daily, when it could be given to people instead.

Some of our new housemates had been sleeping rough for a long time before turning to squatting and finding this crew. Others were people who wanted to tackle the problem from within, instead of adding to it. We had all come together from different backgrounds, yet we all made one big team that was fighting for the same thing.

The squatting rules Tom had taught us on the first night in Finchley Road became rules we all knew by heart and had to put into action daily.

Remember rule number 3: always squat with a group of people; it's safer, better, and more fun. One of the guys, Leo, worked daytime as an engineer/electrician and as our saviour at night-time, managing to get us running water and electricity wherever we went. There was a guy with a van who helped us move the mattresses and other things whenever we had to move. And there were people who knew where the best bins were, what time they got filled, and what exactly you could get from where.

Remember law number 4: find out who owns the place, and try to find an agreement with the owner. Once again, nobody seemed to care about this nightclub, and despite Leo, Tom, and others trying to contact with the supposed owner, they got no replies.

And at all times, know the law. As a squatter, you have more rights than you think you might. Knowledge is power, and it will determine how long you're gonna be able to survive this lifestyle.

Overall, life was good. We were all sleeping together in a big room above the glass stairs, which I assume had once been used for dancing. We had all our mattresses around this old dance floor, with sleeping bags and duvets to keep us warm. Every morning I would wake up to the sounds of waves on the Thames and could see how the water moves; every evening I would go to sleep with the lights of the HSBC building in Canary Wharf shining on me, with the calming sounds of the waves. The only thing that was missing was the sound of dolphins in the background, then I could have released an album called 'The Beautiful Calming Night Sounds for your Resting Soul'. I was surprised that you could find peace in the middle of Canary Wharf, but apparently you can.

A lot of the times we would be hanging out on the sofa, in awe of the view, and knowing that, legally, none of us could ever afford to have a home with such amazing surroundings. Most people on this earth couldn't. Yet somebody on this earth owned this property and wasn't giving a toss about it, just leaving it unused and abandoned. How bizarre.

It was the beginning of November, and the weather was getting cold and wet. Our place could have accommodated at least one hundred people desperately needing a place to stay, if not more. But unfortunately, you can't just start charity squats, even though they would make sense and are badly needed. Due to squatting's bad reputation, you have to keep your places a secret from the authorities, unless you want to end up on the streets yourself.

Greenwich was also the place where Austin and I became a couple. Back in warm September, when we were hanging out by the Camden Docks, he told me drunkenly that he liked me. All I could do was laugh. I had never been in a relationship before. The most romantic I had been was when I had thought about my gel-haired boy in the Estonian hostel. I had never really attracted much attention from men, probably because I looked like one myself. So, to hear how somebody with a penis say how he liked me, felt pretty unbelievable yet terribly sweet.

Austin was the sunny man of our group. He was always smiling and being active, walking around in his French hat, Camden cowboy shoes, and a light brown leather jacket, no matter how cold it was. Everybody loved him and he loved everyone, too; he befriended and spoke to every single person.

In the evenings, he'd play Bowie on the guitar and tell his funny stories about America. The English always love to hear stories about how messed-up their Western big brother is, their ridiculous healthcare system, the stupid laws on guns, the way they mispronounce words, and even their weird eating habits (such as putting gravy on biscuits!). It makes the English feel better about themselves.

Maybe that was one of the reasons why everybody liked Austin so much. He laughed along with the English when they listened to his American stories, but the more we went around London and became acquainted with the British life, the more we could see the similarities between the two countries.

Austin never told the others that; he just kept laughing with them while they all agreed that America was completely messed-up and England was much better.

I have always been a slightly awkward, reserved type of person. I need time to open up to people and to get used to the environment around me. So, with this friendly, loud American by my side, we made a pretty interesting yet weird duo. I know for a fact that it was his social skills that kept us alive in this ever-changing squatting life, because he knew everything about everything, and the love we had for each other dragged me along for the ride.

I've never really been good at chit-chat; I am an Estonian, after all, and we hardly speak regardless of the situation. I prefer to observe, and enjoy silence. We have a saying in Estonia: Talking is silver, silence is gold. But in this new environment, I came to understand that if I wanted to stay alive, I had to change my mindset to 'Talking is gold, chit-chat is gold. If you are silent, you will be considered an arrogant weirdo,'

For the first time in my life, I forced myself to make small talk. 'Hey, how are you?' became a question I regularly asked without actually listening to the answer. Talking about the weather became a topic for long discussions. Even though the sentiments are always the same – the weather is always shitty, cold, and wet – the English still love to still talk about it, wonder why it is the way it is, have a little whine, and then drown themselves in a milky tea or a pint of beer.

I learned a lot during this time, from the moment I woke up to the moment I went to sleep. Law and human rights were one thing; Excel and selling skills at work, second; and trying to fit into the English life without looking like a weird immigrant was another. I'd like to think that I did pretty well at the first two, but I found the talking easier said than done.

The fact that my mind stopped working completely when Austin was around didn't make it any easier for me to blend in with other people. But fortunately, our sunny boy had his social skills covered since birth (he was American, after all – the land of everything), and he kept me on board. Whenever I would come across as unintentionally and inexplicably bizarre, he would joke, 'She's an eastern European, they don't speak English.' And everybody would nod their heads, smile, and say they understood. Then they would have discussions about how complicated the English language could be, while I was quietly blushing in the darkness. Little did they know that my weirdness wasn't caused by my language skills, but due more to my non-existent social skills.

I also learned that in England, Estonia is considered to be eastern Europe. This was something completely new to me; in Estonia, we consider ourselves as northern, one of three Baltic countries, a blend of the north and the east. These three nations - Estonia, Latvia, Lithuania - have not much in common with the other eastern European countries, besides the USSR history and the large Russian communities we still have, due to that period. But in England, northern Europe consists of four countries (Norway, Sweden, Finland, and Denmark), and eastern Europe seems to blend into one big Slavic blob, no matter where these countries actually are.

Whenever people mentioned me coming from eastern Europe, I just smiled. East for me meant Russia and the countries below the Baltics. At first, I thought they were joking, and I didn't have a good comeback. I didn't know how to speak up and explain myself to these new people, not only about the geography but in everything. I was terribly awkward, quiet, and aloof.

Fortunately, the people that were around me were nice enough to understand this little weird girl, and Austin the sunny boy was so chatty that he talked enough for both of us.

Although we had a million-dollar view (if not more), Leo, Tom, and others had kept their eye on a business warehouse in Surrey Quays and were planning to move there. The new place was going to be huge, and there were plenty of people that were going to join us. One of the groups that we called The Lithuanians (because they were four Lithuanians) went there for a week to test the waters. A few days later, they gave us the green light that the place was safe and habitable. I was sad to leave our glass nightclub, but I understood that for better and safer living conditions we couldn't stay in our dance hall squat forever.

Our new home was a two-storey office space / warehouse, and we entered the building from the office side, through the side door. The moment you went in, you found yourself in an enormous lounge. The rooms that had previously been used as offices became our bedrooms, and these were given out on a first-come-first-served basis. Austin and I got one of the smallest rooms in the house, but it was still bigger than any room I had ever had before. My grandmother's whole flat was the same size as this damn room! We furnished it with the one mattress and three bags of clothes that we had – our only possessions. But we didn't open the bags yet; you never knew when you might have to run again.

Living in Surrey Quays was one of the best times of my life. In the following weeks, our group got bigger and bigger as people from other squats and places came to live with us. Since the place was so big, and in order to keep it safe, we had to have a big crew. And soon we had about 50-60 people living there.

When our group had previously been mostly English, now we had people from all over the world living with us, all with interesting stories of how they'd got there, why, and when. My everyday curriculum added another topic – cultures. Whatever question I had about the world, there was somebody from that particular place who could answer me. I didn't need Google; all I had to do to get information was walk into the kitchen or lounge and find the right person. It was fantastic.

We even had a dog – a brown Labrador – that belonged to this pink-haired Italian girl. Unfortunately, she was busy working or drinking beer, so a lot of the times the dog had to go and get his love from someone else. That someone else turned out to be Austin. That dog loved him so much that every time Austin patted him, the poor thing got a lipstick. I told you, everybody loved that sunny boy, and I really mean everybody.

About a week after moving into Surrey Quays, we received a letter from the court. *Dear occupiers, you have hereby been notified to attend the court in order to discuss further action regarding the premises. Thank you very much.* Nobody was nervous, nobody really minded. Instead, people were happy that Section 75 had been read carefully and the situation was going to be handled peacefully; Finchley Road had shown us that was not always the case.

Everybody from our group who wasn't busy that day went to court to defend our home and to tell our side of the story. There were around 30 people. I unfortunately couldn't go, as my work condemned taking days off so much that I didn't even dare to be sick. In hindsight, I should have quit my job right that moment when I understood that, but the truth is that I like to work, I like to be busy. So I followed my job rules (as strict and undermining as they were) while others went to save our home.

They did it well. They had followed all the squatters' steps, knew their rights and obligations, and the law was on our side. After spending ten days there, we finally dared to open our bags because we had managed to keep our home. Everybody knew it was only a matter of time until the company would come up with something to get us out. But until then, it was time to enjoy what we had. It isn't often that your home is a business space with a warehouse for skateboarding and you can sleep in an office.

Most of the 'residents' were either students or had a job, but it´s hard to rent a place if you only get paid £6.50p/h, or less. Everybody did their deed during the day. Even Austin found work – he handed out flyers for a comedy club and later became their barman, although his visa didn't actually allow him to have a job at all.

I'm still quite surprised how so many people from such different walks of life managed to live under one roof without any big arguments. I guess the key factor was respect, and understanding that in order to make the situation work and benefit everybody, you had to be tolerant and calm. At the end of the day, we were all working towards the same goal, we were all in the same boat, and if people had started undermining each other, everybody would have drowned.

We were living the type of life that is usually regarded as dirty, messy, antisocial, and perhaps even wrong. Truth be told, though, it was actually quite fun.

8

~

Now, if I may, I will take a minute to talk about my work. After all, I was very happy that I had it. Remembering the struggles of the summer and early autumn where nobody wanted to even hear about me, I was relieved that I finally had a job that was fairly easy and I didn't have to deal with too many complaining customers or scrub shit off toilets (I already lived in enough places where I had to see that). All I had to do was talk people into buying stuff they didn't need. The job was completely unsuitable for me, that's for sure, but for some reason I had gotten it. And I was happy. Confused, and definitely not the greatest worker there, but happy.

We had a small group. Besides me, there were only nine of us working in the company's three London branches. Only three of the girls were English; everybody else was from around the world, including two Estonians who were already there when I joined. I think the only reason I got hired was due to my nationality. Perhaps the manager thought that I would be just as hard working, smart, and able to make even crap look saleable, just like the other Estonians there. I'm sorry to have proven him wrong.

My job was to be a shop assistant nine hours a day, five-six times a week. All I had to do was sell people bags for their laptops, mobile phones, and sports gear, explaining how everything was durable, waterproof, and amazing. Two words I used a thousand times per day (as taught by the supervisor) were: amazing durability. The bags were good, but I had zero faith in them myself. And I simply couldn't understand how anyone could spend over £100 ON A BAG.

If anyone wanted to know real durability, I had carried the same Sainsbury's plastic bag, full of my clothes, with me since August. By December, I had lived in four different places, but I still had that same bag with me. Now THAT's some amazing durability – and it hadn't cost me a penny.

Of course, I couldn't tell that story to the clients at work. To them, I offered the sales pitch I had been taught in my first two weeks and that I had reluctantly, eventually, started to use. I knew that I wasn't selling bags due to my great sales pitch or convincing personality. Everybody knew it. I managed to sell bags only because it was almost Christmas time, and everybody who knows anything about sales, retail, or human psychology, knows that you can even sell a piece of shit for a good price during the festive season.

There were two people at work who knew I was squatting. I didn't want anybody else to know. Mona, a German woman who reminded me slightly of my mom, worried about me a lot. I had told her about my living arrangements one time after she mentioned how much junk I ate. It was true; I was munching, constantly, on the worst stuff ever.

'Do you ever eat normal, homemade food?' she asked me, looking concerned. The answer was no. The last time I'd eaten a warm, healthy meal was in the summer when Bobby still cooked for both of us. Once our friendship turned sour, so did his food and my eating habits. Even though the oven at our office warehouse was working, I didn't trust it to cook anything substantial.

One time, I bought a bag of potatoes to fry and boil – every Estonian knows that without potatoes, you can't call a meal a meal. But people in the kitchen didn't understand my love for potatoes and the versatility of this glorious vegetable. I became the 'Potato Girl'. Even Austin started calling me that. I didn't mind the nickname, but I didn't want to cook anything in that kitchen from then onwards. And the only thing I knew how to cook was potatoes, in five different formats.

Mona was too baffled, too worried to even say anything. She'd read the news every morning on the way to work, and every time she saw an article about another squat violently destroyed by the police, she'd run to me to make sure I was still alive. 'Oh, this is horrible! This is so dangerous! Is this your place? Look what the police are doing!' she'd always say to me. Perhaps she felt some sort of motherly affection towards me, the starving, homeless weirdo. Who knows?

The only other person who knew what was happening in my life was Mari, one of the other Estonian girls at work, and the only Estonian friend I had in London. When Lemmi had left in the summer, I had completely submerged myself in the English language, laws, and culture. Even though I loved it, wanted it, had worked hard to get it, it still felt like a blessing to have somebody around who understood your childhood jokes, slang words, and silly country myths.

In my daily life, I had to keep that part of me hidden; it was unnecessary and difficult for others to understand. But with Mari, it all came out. She loved it, too. She had been living in England for three years and was completely Anglified. Before me, she hadn't heard Estonian slang, words, or stories in over three years. It was beautiful. To her, I was the crazy, local girl, who spoke funny tales from home and lived an adventure; to me, she was the good angel who was warm and laughed at my silly jokes. In each other, we found home away from home.

I even told my mom about my newfound love. My whole family was quite surprised to hear about my *BOY*friend. Due to my boyish look and lack of men in my life, they had all considered me gay. 'And where do you live? How's life?' my mother asked.

'Oh, life is wonderful. And we're living in a big, beautiful castle,' I told her.

'Ahah,' she said as she hung up the phone, dismissing this like a teenage romance. I never told her that we were *actually* living in a big, beautiful castle. And I left out the fact that we were sharing it with about 50 other people, the castle was an abandoned building, and we were sleeping on the floor. With Austin, I couldn't have cared less where I did or didn't sleep.

Oh my God, was I in love with him. Sometimes, when selling rich people their lousy bags, I imagined talking about my boyfriend instead.

I could see my boss' sending me disapproving looks when I was wandering around the shop, dreaming. Everybody at work was great at selling, organising Excel sheets and shop windows, while looking flawless themselves. On the other hand, I washed myself perhaps once a week (one of the girls was a student at Goldsmith's and sometimes we could take a shower there on Saturdays), my clothes once every few weeks, and my greasy head was constantly thinking about something else besides work. I wouldn't have cared even if the boss had fired me on the spot. Come to think of it, I never really understood why he didn't.

9

~

It was 16th of December – my sister's birthday. In Estonia, I would have woken up eating cake and singing Happy Birthday to my little munchkin, then made her go to school, while chilling out in PJs in my warm, cosy home. After school, we would have gone to eat pizza, given her a gift and, overall, had a merry, jolly time all day long.

But that day in London's Surrey Quays, I woke up at 7am to Leo screaming out the window from his room next to us, 'There's people living in here! You can't do that! It will take time! There's people in here!'

Confused and still half asleep, I got up and went to the window.

WOW!

There were about five police cars, 30+ policemen, and dogs waiting for us outside, desperate to get us out that very moment. They were standing in the rain with their dogs barking, ready to attack; red and blue lights were flashing, and they were speaking into their walkie-talkies. One of the policemen kept repeating into a megaphone in his low monotonous, robotic voice: 'Leave the premises immediately. You must leave the premises immediately. We will force our way inside in ten minutes. Leave the premises immediately. We will force our way…' He kept going and going.

Within seconds, I had learned a new English word – premises. I was in one. And I had to get out of it as soon as possible.

It was like a final scene from an action film, where the cops were finally about to capture the bad men in a dramatic way. Only this time, I was one of the bad guys. And this wasn't a film. This was my life, and it was happening at that very moment.

I quickly woke Austin up, hastily put on some random clothes, and ran through to Leo´s room. He was having talks/screaming competition with the police from the window, trying to save us some time and attempting to handle things in as civil way civil as possible. And it was true: you simply can´t get 50/60 people out of a huge house in just ten minutes, especially when some of them are sleeping on the other side of the building, away from the noise.

But the policeman kept going like a broken record about leaving the premises immediately. Did they not understand we were working on it already? I saw everybody running around chaotically, as I rushed about myself, trying to gather up what I could. It didn't matter what was whose, as long as it got taken with us.

All of a sudden, there was a loud sound of breaking glass. I was running towards our room when, suddenly, everybody froze. The main door had been bashed in. The big entrance doors leading straight to the lounge that we never used had been destroyed with such force that all the glass walls next to them had shattered, too. The police were inside. They had definitely taken less than ten minutes, despite their promise.

It became like a movie scene; like something in a rioting prison. About 30 policemen ran in along with their barking dogs, heading to different floors, kicking in doors and screaming at people to move faster, checking every nook and cranny; the dogs looked like they were a second away from attacking everybody; people were running around like headless chickens, grabbing everything they could; mattresses were being thrown from rooms onto the ground floor lounge, to be picked up by others waiting downstairs.

I had never expected to witness something like this in real life. It was so surreal that when Austin came with our packed bags, even he couldn't help but laugh nervously in disbelief – and that boy is paranoid about anything to do with the authorities. This was our LIFE, although it looked more like a war movie set. I felt as though I was still asleep and having a nightmare.

Outside in the rain, amongst the many police cars, was our van. Everybody was throwing mattresses and bags into the vehicle as quickly as possible, acting on emotions, confusion, and policemen screaming into their ears, instead of logic and common sense. The rain was so heavy that everybody was soaking wet within minutes, and it was hard to make sense of what had just happened.

Our big group was being divided into many smaller groups. Austin and I, the Lithuanians, Italian and her dog, plus another ten people, went to a squat in Elephant & Castle. Frankly, I don't know where the others went. Everything happened so quickly that we didn't really have time to talk to each other. As long as they said they were good, it was fine.

I could hardly think that day after the morning's happenings, but I did manage to sell one or two bags, somehow. And I managed to pull off an excited and happy voice when I called my sister and wished her a happy birthday. She didn't need to know what trouble her sister was up to.

10

There was a house in Elephant & Castle that had been a squat for about a decade. By the time we got there at Christmas 2011, it had already stood for many years. As of 2020, it´s still standing. There were about eight people there, and they had a very good understanding with the owner who had generously let them stay in the house. The rules were simple: take care of the building and keep the looters away; in exchange, you can stay rent-free.

We arrived at Elephant & Castle like bunch of refugees from Syria – wet, cold, confused, but happy to be alive. Unfortunately for us, though, due to that rule with the owner, we couldn't stay in the house for too long. We understood. Anyway, we liked our big group so much that we wanted to find a new place where we could all live together again.

For two weeks, we lived in that living room, mattresses all put next to each other, bunched together like sardines in a can. Christmas was approaching, so a lot of our crew went off to see their families.

The house was quite quiet – not because there were fewer people, but because we were supposed to be feeling merry and jolly at that time of year, yet none of us did.

In our house, nobody mentioned the festive season. There were no presents exchanged, no Christmas songs sung, no big meal eaten, and no tree lit up. As a matter of fact, everybody pretended like it was just any other time in winter. Don´t get me wrong. I didn't really mind, because I've never been big on Christmas. Nevertheless, I tried to ask work for time off so that I could go to Estonia and spend it with my family, but they said, 'If you go away for that time, don't ever come back.' So I stayed in London. Because I like to work, and I *especially* love to sell bags.

As I was spending my first Christmas away from my family, I didn't really mind being in a stinky-socks-and-weed-infused, cold building instead of a lovely, warm home. I spent the 24th of December working, and to my surprise, it was one of the busiest days of the year. People (especially desperate men) came running to the shops and were willing to buy almost anything in order to get that last-minute gift. I didn't even have to say hello.

It was a sad environment back in the building, though. Holidays mean everywhere is quiet and, whether you want it or not, your mind drifts off to thoughts you usually manage to hide away for the rest of the year. Christmas is a family holiday. For a whole month, every poster, every advert, screams family fun and love in your face wherever you go or whatever you do.

Supposedly, this is the time we all should be happy and united, and miracles could happen. But if you happen to be away from your family or don't have your loved ones near you, it is the loneliest time of all – no matter who else is there. And miracles don't happen. Every advert, every poster, just reminds you of everything that you're missing out on, and rubs your sadness and emptiness in your face even more.

So there we were, on the evening of 24th of December, a bunch of us dirt-broke squatters chilling in a living room, all away from our families, drinking cheap wine and expired Super Malt we had gotten from the skips. Our group that was usually cheerful and active was very quiet that night. Nobody felt like talking, even though the wine tasted good. We had all drifted off to somewhere else but here. I drifted off to a place I hadn't thought of in months, since I met Austin – Estonia.

In Estonia, Christmas is celebrated on the 24th of December. That day, people go to graveyards and light candles for their lost loved ones; some people even go to church. You spend the day making big meals – sauerkraut, verivorst (blood sausage), cranberry sauce, sült (meat jelly), pumpkin salad, and of course, the heart and soul of every Estonian table –potatoes. Heaps and heaps of potatoes. All the bowls are filled with gingerbread cookies and clementines. For me, Christmas smells like clementines.

The 24th is usually celebrated quietly with your closest family (25th is for the distant relatives). People eat till they can't move, and watch silly Christmas crap on TV. Home Alone *is always on.*

All of a sudden, there are three options:

1. *The father has to go 'somewhere'.*
2. *Your grandmother/grandfather has to go 'somewhere'.*
3. *Family friend/neighbour has to go 'somewhere'.*

About ten minutes after that person has gone 'somewhere', you hear the doorbell. Oh, who is it? Is that Santa Claus? Yes, yes, it is!

'Ho- ho- ho, are there any good children in this household?' the mysterious Santa Claus asks, as they're making their way inside carrying a big bag full of presents on their back and a red dressing gown (that, weirdly, is like one your father/mother has, but let's pretend we don't see it). This is a REAL Santa Claus from Lapland in Finland, and he/she has nothing to do with a member of your family who just left a second ago… to go somewhere.

'Ho-ho, I come from Lapland, far, far away, and I am very tired. May I sit?' The Santa Claus sits on a chair usually right next to the

tree, and for the next few minutes has to hear all about the kids' year, just to make sure they really have been good. Then, Santa opens his bag. Kids go wild.

'Alright, this one is for Jaanus!' Jaanus is ecstatic. What's he gonna get this time? Has he actually been good? The excitement is killing his little body.

There are no free meals in this world; Estonians learn that early. In order for Jaanus to get his present, he has to do something. Recite a poem, sing a song, dance, act, whatever. Do something. It's easy for the kids, cause they've spent the whole of December learning poems and songs by heart at schools and kindergartens, preparing for this moment.

'You do want to get presents, don't you? You want Mommy to be proud of you, don't you? You want Santa to come to you this year, don't you? Then read and remember these poems for your dear life!' Estonian kindergartens are fun.

It's a different story for the adults. They are usually too stressed and overworked (in order to afford those presents, somebody has to make money) that they can barely remember their own name or a reason for existing. This is the usual scenario:

As Jaanus is singing a third verse of a song (out of key and waaayy too loud), Santa Claus says 'Alright, alright, well done, my boy. Here is your gift, and because you were such a good boy and sang the whole song, here is a present for your Mommy, too.' Jaanus is so proud for being a good boy, and his mom is relieved that she didn't have to embarrass herself in front of her family and a fictional Santa. She still wants to shag Santa later, you know.

Elderly people usually sing a song/recite a poem from the horrible wartime – one they learned when they were ten years old yet could never forget because its sad lyrics became their actual life. Everybody cries. Nobody dares to say anything, out of politeness. This repeats till the year that they die.

Once all the presents are given out, Jaanus has lost his voice from all the horrible singing he's done to get his four presents, everybody's cried two times and been embarrassed many more. Santa has to leave, to give other kids their presents. The reindeers need to move so they don't freeze to death or die of boredom while Santa is listening to your crap. 'Thank you, Santa! See you next year!' Kids are so happy. Adults are happy, too, because now they can proceed with a normal night. 'Ho-ho, be a good boy!' Santa leaves through the door. The reindeers are out the back; you will never see them.

About ten minutes later, the father/neighbour/grandmother returns.

'Oh, you just missed him! Santa Claus was here! But look, I was so good I got your present as well!' Jaanus happily declares to the freshly returned.

'Oh no, what a shame! Perhaps I'll see them next year.'

People keep eating, and will soon go to bed. The tradition says (Estonians don't really believe in God, but they believe in the ancient spirits and your lost elders) not to clean your table that night and leave all the food out, because once you've gone to bed your lost loved ones can come and take part in your Christmas meal, too. Or maybe it's the mice? Whatever and whoever is eating the food, 24th of December is the night that they can.

That would have been my night in Estonia. I would have eaten homemade food till I felt sick, and pretended for my little sisters that Santa really does come to your home and bothers to listen to your crap. He even congratulates you with presents for doing so.

But in order to keep my job, I stayed in London. I ate the 'meal deal' sandwiches from the bin, washed them down with expired lemonade and red wine, counting down the hours for this holiday time to end so that I could feel normal again. Everybody around me felt the same.

Without family and loved ones, Christmas truly is the loneliest time of all – no matter who else is there.

We were out of Elephant & Castle before New Year's Eve, even though we still didn't really have anywhere to go. Once again, our group that was already divided enough got torn apart even more. Every day, we spoke to our scattered crew about possible squats and new places but nothing was certain. Nobody was sure about the future, nothing was definite. On top of that, the government started changing the laws regarding skipping and more and more supermarkets started locking their bins, which made it impossible to get food from certain places. Usually, we knew about five skips where we could get food, but during the following weeks it changed to two, on the good days three. With that, the hardest time of my squatting life began.

It was January, the month that everybody hates the most. It's dark, cold and wet; everybody's poor after Christmas and New Year. But it is an especially difficult month to get through if you don't have a home and you live on quick noodles, Tesco meal deals, booze, and haven't slept properly for weeks.

To be very honest, that next month is a complete blur to me. Within the space of four weeks, we lived in about five places. I would call Austin every day after work and he would tell me the new address where we were going to stay for the night. Every night was different, every place looked the same.

Keeping in touch with the others and having the experienced Lithuanian quartet do their work, we found ourselves in this place in Catford – a small, detached house with no furniture, electricity, or water. The toilet was full of old shit and papers from Lord knows when. We slept there for about a week and the talented Lithuanian boys managed to give us electricity, although I'm not sure if it was a good idea. Yes, we could charge our phones and listen to music, but we could also see all the dirty floors that we were sleeping on, walls that were crumbling due to mould and humidity, and a toilet that was not only full of faeces already, but where some diseases had started taking form as well. It was grim. I started doing my business in the local McDonald's instead, and prayed before falling asleep that the walls would still be up when I woke in the morning.

Another place we stayed was near St. John's station. The house was small and full of old, dirty, broken furniture. It seemed like the people that had lived there previously had run off abruptly, leaving their ashtrays full of half-smoked cigarettes and the sink full of unwashed dishes. We always wondered what had happened there, but I guess we'll never know.

Every time the lights were turned off, it would take approximately fifteen seconds for the mice to come out. We could hear them running around next to us on the floor and tables, eating whatever they could, including our clothes and bags. Even my amazingly durable Sainsbury's bag had holes in it, due to these lovely mice. Austin could handle a lot, but he hated the rodents, so he'd put David Bowie on to distract us from their squeaking – not that it ever actually did.

For a while, we even stayed in an abandoned pub somewhere in south London. God knows where that place was. I was too exhausted to know what was going on by that point, and even though I remember sleeping there near the bar (once again, it had everything but liquor), I can't say more about this or the other few places we stayed at. I was too tired to exist half of the time by then.

Besides travelling around London and sleeping wherever possible, I still had to go to work every morning and be part of 'normal life'. And this all started taking its toll on me. I wasn't awake even when I was awake. I became one of those people that can fall asleep anywhere within seconds. A tube journey that lasted for more than two stops meant an opportunity to sleep for at least five minutes. Instead of eating, I'd sleep during my break time at work in the back of the store. As soon as I sat down, I dozed off. I couldn't help myself. I became a zombie. A walking dead, barely awake, human-looking existence.

Besides Mona and Mari, nobody else at work knew that I squatted, so I'm quite surprised that nobody ever said anything about my zombie-like appearance. Maybe they thought it was my natural state? Or that I was sick? People either care too much or not at all; there's no middle way whatsoever. Funny creatures.

I became very good at orienting with maps. Since I woke up almost every morning in a new place, the tube map became my best friend. I worked five-six times a week and the other one/two days I tried to go skipping and be as helpful for my squatting mates as possible. They took care of me most of the week, finding places to live, so it was the least I could do. I was still considered the quiet, slightly weird, and distant one in the group, but my behaviour was excused as me being a cold eastern European. Actually, all I needed was a good sleep and a warm meal – that would have done the trick, too.

One might wonder why I didn't start renting a place when squatting got so bad. I obviously had some money saved by then, and the stress of not having a solid home, eating crappy snack food, and not sleeping enough, were obviously taking a toll on me. So, why didn't I?

Oh my, I hate myself for the answer. But there was really only one reason.

I didn't leave squatting because of Austin and the enormous love I had for him, even though it was slowly killing me and, due to that, our relationship. I was so into him that I simply couldn't imagine spending a night without him. Sleeping on a cold stone floor with no pillow felt better than a soft bed, as long as he was there with me; icy air was warmer, hearing mice run around us just a white noise; and the weight of stress on my heart felt much lighter as soon as I saw him. I know myself how ridiculous it sounds, yet I couldn't help myself. Not being near him, not feeling his arms around me, hurt my mind, so I decided to suffer physically instead and live in those dirty, unstable, even dangerous places.

I had started squatting due to lack of money, then out of principle and due to the cool people I met. When I understood that I couldn't keep up with the lifestyle and its rules, I stayed out of love. You might not have to pay rent, but you have to pay shitloads of attention when you decide on this choice of living.

Austin was having the time of his life, although he too was struggling with the living arrangements and the dirty mice constantly running around us. He was stronger than me to fight with all of it, but unfortunately, I couldn't keep up. Having to be two different people in 24hrs got tiring. I should have left. But I couldn't.

In 2011, the rules were that as an American, your UK visa lasted for only six months. After that, you could travel around Europe for another three months. Austin had until March before his visa expired, then he'd have to leave the UK. He decided to hitchhike through Calais towards France and then Berlin, before going back to the States. That meant we had two months left to adventure or suffer together (depending on which angle you looked at it), then go our separate ways.

I didn't fancy staying in England without him, so I decided to go back to Estonia in March. The fact that our life together, our love, had an expiry date made things easier and the punches softer, because we knew exactly when it would end.

I told you, everybody who knew him loved him, and so did I. Oh, I loved him more than myself, and I was ready to follow him wherever the night and time took us, no matter how scary the neighbourhood or how dirty the place.

I decided to quit the job after four months of being there, and I'm sure they were happy about my leaving. Christmas time was over, sales had gone down rapidly, and in my exhausted state of mind I could hardly exist, let alone talk people into buying things. I just wanted to spend the final months with Austin before he returned to Seattle, and we both knew it would be years until we saw each other again.

But for now, we had London.

There had been rumours going on for a while that a council estate in Woolwich Arsenal had about fifty flats, with half of them empty. Throughout the weeks we were touring around south London, our comrades had tested the waters once more, liked what they saw, and by the end of January we took our few bags to Woolwich Arsenal. It was only me, Austin, and the multi-talented Lithuanian quartet. Everybody else declined to come, as it was too far for them to travel to work or school every day.

Woolwich Arsenal was in zone four, but it was pretty nice. It had a DLR station, a big, buzzing high street with lots of shops, a little green town square, and heaps of chicken and chip shops.

Although there were pretty nice-looking restaurants in this Woolwich area, and every shop you needed was right there on the high street, we hardly got to see that part. Our estate was located behind the fancy buildings and beautiful streets, away from the hustle and bustle. And it was a different type of life there. The council estate was made up of huge, grey, cold, concrete buildings, all next to each other, creating their own little section. The streets were dirty, walls covered in angry, vulgar graffiti, and there was a definite possibility of getting stabbed/robbed by anybody who walked past. This council estate section reminded me a lot of the 'nice hotel' full of syringes and weird substances where I'd played with my friends as little kids back in Estonia.

I have never lived in a place before where I'd had to watch over, under, behind, and in front of my shoulder at the same time as I was walking to/from home. In that council estate in Woolwich, I had to. There were kids running around outside selling drugs, and they'd creep up to you every time you were outside.

'Oy, you there, oy! Do you smoke? You... like stuff?' They were only about eleven, maybe younger.

'No.' I'd try to get away as fast as possible.

'Pussy,' they'd say, their bodies fidgety and eyes already searching for another victim or any possible danger. This would happen every day, and watching them getting high on their own supply while trying to sell it to you, did not get easier within time. When I was eleven, I had been obsessed with MTV and VH1, dancing to every music video and dreaming my life away. These kids didn't seem to have dreams at all, no aspirations and no love. Maybe TV isn't completely bad then, eh?

We started living in one flat on the second floor, although it looked like the whole four floors with its twenty+ flats were all empty. We never saw any neighbours and we never heard any other living activity, besides ourselves and the creepy children and gangs outside. We knew there were more people living in the building, for sure, but the estate was huge, making it feel like the whole place had been ghosted. The only indication of other people was when you saw fresh bloodstains on the stairs and/or in the lift. Besides that, there were never any sounds or movement.

Soon enough, our group grew bigger. New people came in, and we were then using four flats from the estate, all next to each other. Due to the place being big enough and having a very eery effect, we mostly stayed together in the middle, main flat.

There were a few times in the Woolwich Arsenal when we were visited by the police, but we were never scared; the skilful Lithuanian quartet always knew the right things to say or do.

About a week before Austin and I were supposed to leave, we got a court order. I had never seen anything so formally thorough before. It had about fifteen pages – fourteen more than what was needed. The first page was a formal court invitation, with the time and place of the hearing. The rest of the pages were basically saying, in detail, that the whole premises seemed to be 'infested with eastern Europeans', who didn't seem to have a job and were 'just squatting, destroying the premises'.

I had never read before how horrible eastern Europeans could be and what they – WE – were apparently doing to the place. We all read it, laughed at it, and were shocked by the supposed happenings, all at the same time. The English in our group found it hilarious to read how they were being considered unemployed, destructive eastern Europeans threatening this building and the nation.

I wasn't laughing, though. I had never seen words like these put together in this way against a certain group of people, and didn't know what to think of it.

Out of the fifteen people we had living in the house, only six were eastern Europeans, one was American, and the rest were English. The part that made me the saddest was the claim that we were 'destroying the premises'. We hadn't broken anything since we arrived. As a matter of fact, we were like cleaners working for free, scrubbing bird shit off the balcony, dusting the floors and the little furniture that was there, while keeping it safe from the gangs and drug dealers lurking outside. Some of us had jobs, some of us didn't; so their assumption that we were all unemployed looters was totally wrong.

Honestly, nobody really cared too much about the court case. Everybody living there had been to court many times before and knew the drill. Most of them also felt unsafe living in the estate and had started thinking about new options, so getting kicked out by the authorities was not going to be that bad.

Austin left for France early March, and a few days later, I flew back home to Estonia. When I returned to London four months later and saw the Lithuanians again, they said they had easily won the court case. The whole council estate was in such a bad condition and the area so rough that the judge seemed surprised that anybody even lived there at all, whether paying rent or not.

As they did not want to be surrounded by eleven-year-old drug dealers, though, the guys had decided to leave the place themselves. Once again, the crew got smaller, with people going in different directions, surviving in their own way, finding their own paths.

I was done with that lifestyle forever. All the laws regarding squatting had changed, and not in favour of the occupants. Section 75 and its peaceful ways of sorting out the situation had begun to mean nothing. The rights as a squatter were now close to zero. People who don't know much about this lifestyle still seem to consider squatters to be looters and hobos, somewhat second-class citizens, which is a real shame. I met some of the most interesting and smartest people during this squatting period, and we treated every single place we stayed at like our home, cleaning and protecting it. So all these assumptions about squatters are a damn shame.

In the meantime, homelessness in the UK is still growing, just like the rent and property prices. Skipping has been made illegal, and more and more supermarkets are locking their bins along with its heaps of edible food. It's a shame, really. The people that have the power over these things don't even realise what they are deciding on. For them, it's a rule that doesn't change anything for them. But for somebody else in need, these changes could mean everything.

In that last nine months, I had lived in about thirteen places – twelve of them squats.

It took me many years before I saw Austin again, and I haven't seen any of the other squatting people since that time. But I guess that's life.

Now I needed to go back to Estonia, eat, sleep, and become a person again… and take a long, hot shower.

11

I spent the first few weeks at home sleeping, eating, and taking long, hotter-than-hell showers. My grandmother was happy that I was back and she fed me all the sweets and potatoes she could buy from the shop, just as she had done fifteen years before. If I wasn't busy stuffing my face with food, I was sleeping – on a bed. I have to admit, it felt weird and even slightly uncomfortable, to be sleeping on a soft surface again.

For the past year, the softest thing I had slept on was Austin's belly, and even that had been pretty bony in the end, so I had gotten used to raggedy places. But it didn't take me too long to get accustomed to the 'normal' life again; I suppose it's always easier to get used to luxury than poverty. Still, I began to hug and kiss my grandmother, to show my appreciation for the fact that we had these things, understanding now that a soft, clean bed and a warm shower was not available to everybody.

She thought I had gone crazy living in Auschwitz –in her head, every place outside of your own home is a torture, and showing your emotions and love to your close ones is not something you do in Estonia. Despite being cool, my grandmother is still an ex-USSR woman who was forced to keep her emotions undercover for so long that she's lost them all now. I hugged and kissed her as she ran awkwardly to the shop to buy some more ice cream so I could eat my feelings instead of expressing them, like a normal person does.

I come from Pärnu, south west Estonia. We call it the capital of summer, due to its long, white, sandy beaches and the Baltic Sea. Despite being the third biggest city in the country, it is actually so small that the English would call it a village. To give you a better understanding of this little country of ours, imagine Tallinn as New York, where all the foreign stuff happens, and Pärnu is like Florida, with its long beach, sexy babes, and tanned pensioners. It's mostly alive from May-September, the prime summertime. In the winter, the only thing to do there is drive a car on the frozen Baltic Sea and get drunk in bars.

But as soon as the ice and snow start melting in April, you see the party people arriving. During summertime, you're lucky to hear Estonian language spoken at all. Mostly it's the Finnish pensioners who have come for their spa and mud bath procedures, beach holidays, and to spend their evenings drinking beer and visiting karaoke bars. Others are the Russian grandmothers walking their little barking and biting pugs, while gossiping about everyone around them in a loud voice. In Russian, of course. Despite living in Estonia for more than fifty years, they have never learned the language – partly because of its complexity, but mostly because they still believe in the USSR and the power of their Holy Father, Vladimir Putin.

I returned to Pärnu in late March, when it finally starts getting warmer again. Despite the soon-to-be-buzzing time, I didn't really have anybody to talk to. My friends were scattered around Estonia or Europe, and my family was busy doing their own things. I had got used to talking constantly, selling bags, selling myself, learning how to do small talk, forcing myself to speak even when sleeping, chatting about deep political issues, as well as nothing at all. I had learned to detect awkward silences and kill them in advance with words, ANY words, just to avoid the quietness between two people. I had worked and fought hard to be part of that life, to fit in.

But now, I was back to the old life. And in order to feel good, I had to forget what I had just learned in the last ten months, to shut up and embrace the silence again.

I spent most of my days with my dog, hanging out on the beach and watching my city turn into a naked pensioners' party central, not really sure if I had actually even been to England. Maybe I had just dreamt it all.

Obviously, I couldn't tell my family the type of life I had lived. Could you imagine me telling my grandmother how her granddaughter had lived in abandoned houses, with mice running over her while she was sleeping, eating food from a bin, encountering police raids and court cases? She would have gotten a heart attack! So I kept it all to myself.

I watched every episode of every season of the shows like *Never Mind the Buzzcocks*, *The Peep Show*, and *Vicar of Dibley*, just to hear the English accents and the dark, sarcastic humour again and again. Whenever there were scenes of London in the *The Peep Show*, my whole body melted like the snow outside my window.

The whole of that last year felt like a dream that never happened, and the future didn't matter. I had no idea what to do or where to go. In my head, I was Jeremy, trying to make it in the music business in London; in my head, I was Dawn French telling the word of God to the people in the English countryside. In real life, I was in Estonia, eating potatoes with my dog, while crying in front of my laptop and listening to the half-naked Finnish pensioners singing karaoke songs outside.

'Eva, we gotta go back to London. Too many things were wrong last year, my head wasn't in the right place. We gotta go back. That's where the life's at,' Lemmi contacted me one day. She was living in Tallinn, had taken lots of courses, broken up with her boyfriend (again), and was eager to get back to the big city to test her new wisdom and independence.

She also said how proud she was of me for staying in London that long and for doing the things I had done. Although, knowing her love for cleanliness and organisation, I left out the little facts about me not washing myself for months or sleeping on the floor covered in bird shit and mice. Ignorance is bliss.

'C'mon, let's go. What are you gonna do in Estonia? Nothing!' she kept repeating. Indeed, I hadn't done much else besides watching English TV shows and eating non-stop since I'd returned. But truthfully, there was nothing for me to do in London, either. All I could think about were the times I had been by myself, jobless, penniless, sad. And I was not ready to live through that again.

But Lemmi promised that everything was going to be different this time. After all, we had English CVs now - something that we didn't have the previous year, and which had turned out to be the biggest obstacle in the job field. In her words, we were 'gonna be super-duper, awesome' and 'two tough, independent women'.

I wasn't too sure about that, and I had no real desire to return to London. For me, the whole city still reeked of Austin and reminded me of our good, yet finished, times there. But when the shows that kept me alive had all been watched for a third time in a row and the local beach became crowded with naked old bodies, I had to get out. And since, frankly, I had gotten to know the life in London better than the life in Estonia, I decided to go back to what I knew.

Isn't it funny? Sometimes you can learn more in nine months than you do in twenty years. True story.

I booked a ticket back to London for the end of July, and Lemmi was gonna join me a few days later. She was happy, I was scared – just like we had been a year before.

And damn was my grandmother confused. Why would anybody want to go live abroad if you had the beach right in front of your home?

12

I arrived back in London in July, when the temperature was at its highest and the Summer Olympics were just about to start. The whole town was buzzing extra hard, full of athletes and their fans who, when not in Stratford, were marching around Oxford and Piccadilly Circus, sweaty and tired from the heat, trying to take in as much as they could of this chaotic, central London life.

I had learned before to stay away from Regent Street, especially on the weekends. Unfortunately, though, I hadn't learned that summertime in London is excruciating. All the concrete buildings radiate extra heat, trains feel like saunas, and every lake, pond, or park that exists in the city is overcrowded with warmed-up zombies like me.

It took me only two hours after I landed to be covered in sweat, and along with another hundred tourists in one small tube carriage, I was ready to pass out from the heat. *Why did I have to come to London in the middle of summer when I could have spent it hanging out on the beach? What an idiot.* I was suddenly jealous of all the grandmas and grandpas swimming in Pärnu, eating ice cream, and looking like grilled chicken. I looked like a wet, tired, ugly dog in the big city.

Lemmi joined me a few days later and I could see that she felt the same – it was so hot that even her waterproof make-up was running down her face. She didn't look too excited about coming back to London now.

For the first few weeks, we stayed at my squatting mate Herbert's place in Shoreditch while he was in Germany. On the night of the axe men, he had run to his friend's place and managed to rent a place with the help of a student loan. It was completely affordable, if you didn't eat much. And that wasn't a problem; as Herbert worked as a part-time model, eating was secondary.

I was very excited about living in the east of the city. I had always thought that the Shoreditch-Hackney-Hoxton area was like the L.A. of London, where all the cool, young people and music was. There was a tattoo parlour and a vegan cafe around every corner, and even though I didn't fit into either of these worlds, I wanted to live in Shoreditch and be part of the cool people, hoping some of their awesomeness would rub off on me as well. Well, hope dies last, as they say.

We watched the opening of Olympics together, with a bowl of popcorn, in darkness. That's one thing I like about English summers, though – it gets dark very early. It's the exact opposite to Estonia where it's light for 21 hours a day for three months straight. After some time, your eating and sleeping patterns go down the drain, since your body doesn't know what the hell is going on which, overall, makes you feel like a crazy, fat insomniac. Hence, I prefer darkness; I prefer England.

Lemmi wasn't joking when she said everything would be different this time around. As soon as the opening of the Olympics was over, she sprang into action. She was so determined to make it work this time that it was admirable, yet almost scary, watching her apply for jobs. From the early morning sun until the late evening light, she had her mind fixated on applying for work, being on the phone with employers, fixing her CV, and/or doing trial shifts. I admired her ambition, her organisation.

For me, it was so hot it was hard to breathe, let alone think. I was surviving on cold showers while she was drinking her fourth cup of coffee, sweat dripping onto the keyboard of her laptop, determined to write the best cover letter in the world. But her hard work soon paid off – she found a job at a beauty section, which suited her well. Was she happy? No. Did she have a choice? Not really. But the job paid her bills and added another line on her English CV while she could look for something better. Also, she could be around make-up – something she really loved. Especially when, this time around, it was a mutual decision that she would not use any make-up on me any more.

I was also looking for a job. I remembered that a few people from the squatting days had been working as waitresses and said that even though they got paid less than minimum wage, the tips were so good it was worthwhile. I thought it couldn't be too hard finding a job in hospitality; after all, it was a busy summer, and the city was packed with hungry tourists. Surely somebody somewhere needed an extra pair of hands to help out, right?

Well… as always, it seemed like help was indeed needed in many places, but not from me. I wasn't even surprised at my constant bad luck regarding work. In a weirdly sad way, I had gotten used to being rejected all the time so I didn't take it to heart any more. Fortunately, I had my savings from working in the winter time, so I wasn't as nervous as I had been the previous year. I wasn't rich – definitely not – but as long as I could afford food and pay £100 a week for rent, I was happy.

I didn't find a job as a waitress, but I got a response from a place that was hiring waiting staff for events. I didn't even know what waiting staff meant. I must have clicked on every random link on Gumtree again, because if I had properly noticed the ads of their fancy parties, I would not have even dared to submit my CV to them. They were all proper glamorous, rich, extravagant events – the whole type of shebang that had nothing to do with me. But since they were the only ones that replied to me, I had no choice but to go.

'Please bring a white shirt, tie, black pants, and black polished shoes with you. You can find them in Primark in the men's section. Thank you,' the email said. So, I went and got all that was needed, and I tried them on. I looked like an oversized penguin, like a fish out of water, like a circus artist in an office. In the 30-degree heat, my body felt like it was slowly dying in the suffocating greenhouse my new thick cotton clothes had created. My face was beetroot red, my whole body wet from sweat, and my confidence at minus twelve thousand. Then, I went to the job interview.

The interview went completely differently than I had expected. The boss turned out to be very nice. All we did was talk about bands, while my future boss was sipping on his Yorkshire tea and offering some to me as well. At that time, I couldn't really have cared less about hot drinks, and taking into consideration what was happening under my oversized men's shirt, more heat was the last thing I needed. But in my one year of being in England, I had learned that turning down the offer of tea from an Englishman equals insulting their whole country, the foundation that England has been built on, its people, its culture and history. Little note: I don't care if you are deathly allergic to black tea, milk or hot water, when the English ask if you 'fancy a cuppa, love?', there is only one answer and that is, 'Oh, yes please!'

That's how I got employed for my first events agency work. I had two sips of the milky tea (not out of enjoyment, but politeness), filled out the papers, and was free to go.

It didn't take me long to understand why I had gotten that job so easily, though. Everybody did. You didn't need to have any qualifications, any special skills, an English CV, or anything. Everybody who applied there was offered the job. The only thing that was missing were the actual shifts themselves.

Basically, working as waiting staff/hospitality assistant (same thing, in this case) for an events agency means you have a zero-hour work contract. I signed it without even understanding what it truly meant. Your job is to work at different conferences, parties, and whatever else the rich people decide to do with the help of poor people. There, you put on your oversized men's clothes that make you look like a penguin, and serve fancy food and drinks to them.

The events are always huge, extravagant, and beautiful; men walk around in suits and ties, and women in gorgeous dresses and heels. They eat the tastiest, most delicate food made by grand chefs. The guests smell like money. And the servers are always broke students/youngsters, whose only way of ever seeing anything so nice is by waitering at those grand events. They salivate at the thought of having this food, they see how precisely and delicately all the ingredients are being put together on the plate, they get yelled at by the chefs for not walking fast enough, and they will never get to taste the food themselves.

It's a lovely job to have if you like fancy gatherings and people, but remember – waiting staff's job is usually to wait in the back kitchen where life is nothing like it is in the front. You only go out when there's food and drinks to be served, not to see the show. And you eat the food with your eyes and nose, never really touching it.

The job was unbelievably stupid and so unnecessary in the long run that when I tried to explain to my family what I did, they simply didn't believe that an occupation so pointless and ridiculous would even exist. It took me a long time to make them understand that rich people have events happening every day so the waitresses working at those places can actually make a living out of it. Well, they can pay their rent, transport, and have one Tesco meal deal per day... and then they're out of money. But I guess even that is something.

There are hundreds of agencies that provide staff for prestigious events in London alone; it's a big and competitive field in itself. But my luck in the job field is exceptional. The agency I signed up with was lucky to have three shifts a week to give to its employees. Which meant when I was working, I was overheating, waiting in the back kitchen until the organisers came yelling at you to come out and serve some champagne or canapes. Then I'd go back to the kitchen to wait some more. And if I wasn't waiting at work to be given something to do, I was waiting at home to be invited to an event so I'd have something to do.

No wonder they call the job 'waiting staff'; you spend 90% of your time just hanging about, wondering, waiting.

Once Herbert came back, we had to leave the good, yet terribly expensive, Shoreditch. So, Lemmi and I did what every person wanting to live near Shoreditch/Hoxton area does. If you can, you go live in Bethnal Green. If you can't go to Bethnal Green, you go to Stepney Green. And to the latter we went.

Living in Stepney Green was nice, but the huge difference between my and Lemmi's schedules made living together hard. She woke up early and went to bed early, while I was the exact opposite due to my evening job. The whole time we were sharing a room, it was as if we were living two different lives, walking past each other like strangers. We cared for each other, loved each other, but we always knew that our paths were too different to be walked together. By early October, I moved to a place in Brixton Hill.

I was back in south London once again, although a completely different area to the one where I had lived before. Times were exciting, and I felt like a proper mature person, going to work and renting a room by myself for the very first time. Very exciting, very adult. I had been living in England for almost a year-and-a-half, yet it was the first time it felt like I was settling down and being a good, law-abiding person.

After spending weeks looking for a place in or near Brixton and visiting worse places than any squat I had ever lived in, I had finally found a place in Brixton Hill. It belonged to an older French woman who lived there with her boyfriend, three cats, and a quiet English boy living in the back room. My room was very small. It only had space for one single bed; with a mattress that looked like the springs were going to pop out as soon as you laid on it; a weird broken shelf where I kept... well, nothing, really; a built-in old wardrobe that smelled musty, with its door that promised to come off the moment you opened it. It had also an eye-cringing, blue carpet with some unidentifiable stains left on it from the previous residents.

Doesn't really sound like paradise, does it? Funnily enough, though, this was the best place I could find for my budget. It had a working shower, a stove, four walls that didn't have any remarkable cracks in them, and neighbours that didn't look like they were going to kill me or pimp me out. And I am not - exaggerating. I saw some real gems when searching for a new home. I visited dirtier and more dangerous places than the squats I had lived in – even Woolwich Arsenal seemed nicer.

I moved into my new home at the beginning of October and was determined to make the place my own. After coming back from Estonia in the summer, I had decided to build up my life (or a resemblance to it) in London, as I had nothing else going on anywhere else. Poundland in Brixton became my favourite shop, and my room was a true example of what its franchise can do for the home. I bought different perfumes and sprayed them all on my wardrobe to hide its musty smell. I got some candles to soften the lighting and pictures to distract the otherwise dull, depressing walls. It's a shame Poundland didn't sell carpets or bed sheets, but I'm not complaining.

My sleeping bag was my duvet that I had had with me since the Woolwich Arsenal times. I put my big T-shirts around the old polystyrene pillows I found from the wardrobe, and used them to rest my head on. I didn't have a towel, but I used my clothes to dry myself off after the shower.

The first cold of the autumn started to arrived and, before I knew it, it was November. Despite having a job, I started to struggle with finances again. Poundland was the only place I could afford to buy stuff.

Agencies are always busiest during the time leading up to Christmas, because that's when everybody feels like celebrating and willing to spend even more money on even more pointless things and get-togethers. I was able to work a little more than just three times a week, but all that extra money was spent on things like rent and food. Believe me, buying duvets, pillows, and towels was not on my essentials list.

In order to get food in my belly, I put into action all the things I had learned the previous year regarding skipping. Before going home after my evening shift, I would linger around the two skips at my local Sainsbury's and Tesco had. I soon gave up, though; the skips were locked and the few groceries that were lying around the area were totally inedible due to the never-ending rain.

I also thought about squatting again. There was a place in Brixton Hill that had been a music venue but was now occupied by squatters. I would go past it on the bus every time I went home, and have a look to make sure they were still there. I saw their Section 75 on the front door and imagined myself joining them and living that life again. Unfortunately, they were kicked out few weeks later, before I could do anything.

The place remained empty for a few months but it has been turned into a Tesco store now. The same week I saw the squatters being kicked out, I read in the news about how many homeless people had died due to the UK's cold winter. One of them had frozen to death in front of an abandoned building. If he had entered the building, he would have probably saved his life but been fined, due to his action being illegal. So he decided to follow the law, but paid for it with his life.

It's a shame how upside-down and messed-up the rules of this world are.

Despite being broke and living like a hobo who still had to pay rent, I was actually happy. I didn't mind this kind of living at all. I was grateful to have a clean(ish) and stable place to stay, and I didn't mind working at the events. My biggest worry –loneliness – was not on my agenda this time, because I had Lemmi and Mari to give me company.

Money was a growing problem, but I tried not to let it get me down. It's London, right? Money is always an issue, and everybody's barely getting by. That's just part of life.

It all changed when my mom came to London to visit for a few days.

I was so excited about showing my life to my mom. For the last eighteen months my family hadn't had any idea what I was talking about, what I was doing, or where exactly I was living. They couldn't relate to any of the things I had seen or done, which made our conversations difficult. So, my mom's visit to London for the very first time was a big thing. I wanted to show her my side of life – a side I knew wasn't great, but it was mine. I wanted her to see all the beauty this city had to offer, all the love that I had for it.

I had gotten a place with my own money. I had worked darned hard for that money. I felt the same pride as a little child that has drawn a horse with three legs and no eyes, coloured its hair purple and then declares what a great artist they are. My life wasn't great but, taking into account all the other crap that was around me, I was doing pretty well. All by myself.

My mother stayed for five days. But if she could have, she would have left after the second day. I could see in her eyes how she hated everything she saw. There were too many people in this city, the traffic was chaotic, the lifestyle too hectic. She hated how uncaring people were towards each other; you were surrounded by their uncaring craziness but had to survive in it. She hated how dangerously the tube trains worked and what a loud sound they made.

And the most awful thing of all was the way her daughter lived. That she only had a small, cold, ugly room that had a mouldy smell which she tried to hide with excessive amounts of cheap perfume; that she slept on a bed that was actually unusable; that she didn't even have towels, duvets, or proper pillows. Her daughter was living a life that my mom wouldn't even wish on her enemy, in a city that showed no remorse, love, or help to anybody.

No, my mother didn't *SAY* any of these things to me out loud. But I could read it from her expressions when she saw my room and when we walked around London – it was surprise mixed with disgust. I could hear it from the deep sighs that sounded like her last worrying breaths as she sat on the bed, or had a moment to herself while looking around. She tried to hide her reactions so I wouldn't see. But I saw them all.

She hated the city and she hated my life in it. Every single bit, every nook and cranny. She despised it all.

With every sigh and every look she gave, my heart sank lower and grew heavier, until I felt hollow and dead inside. My three-legged, blind, purple horse turned out to be just a dead scribble on an otherwise beautiful canvas. It was nothing. I was nothing. I had achieved nothing. And I had tried to sugar-coat it and present it as something decent, something beautiful. How pitiful. How embarrassing. I wanted to die.

My mom sugar-coated her feelings and took me shopping for clothes and a towel. I introduced her to Primark – another affordable shop that I visited often, yet one that she hated with all her heart. We went to a restaurant and I ate until I felt like I was going to explode. She bought me heaps of Innocent juices, because the ingredients were supposedly going to make me look better, healthier, and apparently I really needed it.

I also showed her the infamous Poundland shop, but she left after just one minute. 'Do you go to that shop often?' she asked in disgust. I didn't dare to say that I was a regular client whose whole room decorations were from that company. 'No,' I lied to her. 'I just wanted to show it to you, in case you found it interesting.' She didn't. She also couldn't care less about Big Ben, Buckingham Palace, or the Tate Modern.

She did like fish and chips. So, we ate fish and chips five days in a row just to keep her happy. And she didn't say anything bad about my life until years later, when she came to visit me in London again and almost burst into tears seeing that I lived much better.

After those five days, though, I was determined to change my life. It wasn't only my mom's reaction that made me restless, but also because I didn't have £400 to pay for my next month's rent. After doing calculations and taking on more shifts, I still couldn't get the money together.

I also wanted to get out because I realised that the sound I had thought was coming from motorbikes outside every night, turned out to be the boyfriend's snoring. And the reason why the stair carpet was always wet and had weird stains on it, was due to the cats pissing all over it. I had had enough. My room had the same type of stains on it, and for my mental health's sake, I didn't even want to know what had happened there. I just wanted to get out. Those cats were proper knobheads, even though the landlady herself was very nice.

I had heard about a community in New Cross where they were soon going to have a vacancy. All I had to do was wait for few weeks for the place to become available, which was completely doable.

Having lived in hostels before, I decided to spend those few weeks in one again. Living in hostels didn't require any big deposits; you were able to pay by the week, and I didn't mind getting to know new people. I went online to find a place that could offer me accommodation for a bit, and to my surprise, I found one very close to me for a cheap price.

On the 1st of December, I left all the snoring and pissing cats and went to my new home. With my only bag full of clothes, a towel, a sleeping bag, and a guitar, I walked into the next chapter of my life.

I had spent the last eighteen months living like a vagabond, sleeping on floors and not washing myself for months at a time. Throughout that year-and-a-half, I had struggled with money and finding any work. People in my life had come and gone, no matter how much I had tried to hold onto some of them. Loneliness and isolation had become normal, everyday feelings.

I don't know if heaven decided it had played with me enough and finally wanted to reward me for all the shit I had been through. Or maybe it was my mother's desperate prayers for her daughter to have a better life that worked. Either way, I never got to New Cross and its community. As a matter of fact, after I walked into this hostel that December morning, I never really left it. There I found my people, my new home, my family away from family.

In the future, when I was told to 'Go back to where you came from', I went there and got put back together by the beautiful people in it. They are the reason why I stayed in London and found it hard to leave this country after all the shit it started giving me. They are the reason why I love the English, despite all the nasty things some of them love to say about me, my nationality, and my accent.

I went to the Railway.

ACT II

~

I'M AN ALIEN, I'M A LEGAL ALIEN –

I'M AN EASTERN EUROPEAN IN THE UK

13

I have heaps of regrets in my life. Who doesn't? But there are also some things I consider the best things I've ever done and know that they changed my life for the better. I think choosing to live in the hostel in Tallinn was when my real life started. Buying a random ticket and moving to London was when I became an adult. And going to the Railway was what I had to do, where I was supposed to end up.

The Railway was a busy pub with a big beer garden that had a hostel upstairs. I must admit, it wasn't exactly the most beautiful place I've ever set foot in. The stairs to the hostel upstairs were covered in sparkly red linoleum, and the place smelled of greasy chips and cleaning products, which is a perfect recipe for a lovely home. You could see the cracks in the kitchen walls getting bigger with every bass beat that echoed from the downstairs bar.

I was put into a stinky ten-bed boys' room; somehow, I always end up with the boys.

But I fell in love with this place and the people instantly.

The upstairs hostel and downstairs pub formed one big community of English, Irish, and Australians, who all partied and bantered with each other and took care of one another. I felt like part of a group from the very first night I arrived, and from then on my life was never the same. The place was jumping and the people were constantly up to something, so unless I was working, there was no point in even leaving the house. Just like the hostel in Tallinn, it felt like life – along with its quirks – came to me, and all I had to do was open my arms and just embrace it all.

Most of the guys there were from Australia or New Zealand, who were working at construction sites. I came to understand how Aussies are literally everywhere in London. I bet half of the hostels in this city are full of cunts from down under (cunt means a good friend in Oz, apparently!), and they are always happy and ready to party. I swear. These guys can be pretty wild.

From the first night on, I loved all these boys. I didn't mind them burping, farting, snoring, talking about pussy, and having extremely stinky feet. I was enjoying the honesty of existence, even though its smells and sounds sometimes made me gag. But frankly, I ain't the girliest girl myself, and after spending eight months squatting, I can honestly say not much surprised me any more.

The house was awake all the time. Downstairs was a pub that played reggae/ska music until 1am all week, and until 4am on Fridays and Saturdays. You could hear the bass and the dancing people all the way to the second floor, and it was constantly busy and full of people. As the hostages (the long-term hostellers), we had the whole house as our playfield and we mingled with the bartenders and the regulars at the bar. The whole house had a sense of community like there had been in the office warehouse squat, with everybody closely together, respecting each other and hanging out.

I have to admit, though, this place wasn't for the faint-hearted. It was not for people who wanted to come to London for a nice weekend getaway, walk around Oxford Circus, the West End and Buckingham Palace, go shopping in Primark and Harrods, and then come back to sleep in a quiet, clean paradise. Instead, this house was England in its purest form, its ruggedness giving you a real taste of the country you had just bought a ticket to.

There were only two options: you ran out of the hostel as soon as you saw it (that really happened a few times); or you took it for what it was, dove into it head-first and, if you learned to swim, you got yourself a family for life. After a while, I didn't even mind the red, sparkly linoleum floors or the constant grease smell from the kitchen. Actually, the chefs would sometimes even give us free chips, which made up for the constant oil stink.

I had been quite socially awkward in my previous year of living in England, but this year I was in bloom. Although my first reaction to everything was to sit in silence and observe the situation, like any good Estonian usually does, the fun-loving Australian and English boys rarely let me be. They bantered about everything, and if I wanted to stay alive, I had to get used to it and throw the same back at them.

I put to work all the skills I had learned while selling bags and talking half asleep during the squatting days, and became friends with everybody I met. My best friend in the house became Paul, who was sleeping just a bed away from me. He was an Aussie who looked like Donnie Darko and was in love with his guitar and music, taking part in every open mic around town and jamming with everybody he met. My other very good friend became Bianca, an English/Jamaican girl who played ukulele and sang like Billie Holiday, and who I met on our Sunday open mic night.

Together, they took me around town and encouraged me to play at the open mics, too. They had seen my guitar on the bed and wanted me to realise my full musical potential. 'C'mon, this is how you get confident at performing!' they'd always tell me, as they whistled away on their instruments and got heaps of compliments after every performance.

Actually, I did play at the open mic once, but it was pretty bad. Due to my horrendous stage fright, my fingers went jello and I couldn't play any chords. On top of that, I sang Florence and the Machine's *Heavy on my Heart*, forgot the lyrics as soon as I got up on the stage, and just kept repeating how everything feels so heavy in your arms, in your arms, in your arms. For three minutes straight. Nobody even clapped at the end. Bianca and Paul never asked me to play at the open mics again.

I became friends with everybody in the hostel – the Aussies, the English, the Irish, and the Kiwis. The only people I was terrified of were the English girls working behind the bar. They were gorgeous, tough women who weren't afraid to tell you to piss off at any given moment. They were beautiful to look at, all dressed in black, some covered in tattoos, some dripping in jewellery, and all wearing a smile with a side note that says: 'I can punch you to the ground in a second, so don't even give me a reason.'

There were plenty of times on the weekends when I'd see them running around, sorting out the issues outside, while making eight drinks and bantering with three different guys, all at the same time. And they'd always win. It was like the movie *Coyote Ugly* - girls so sexy and smart you couldn't help but stare at them, hoping you can catch up to at least half of what is being said. I felt like a teenage boy from *American Pie,* staring at them. I was terrified.

Of course, they never said anything bad to me as I poured out my last pennies to buy a pint. But I never even dared to open my mouth around them; I knew I'd be crushed in a slang I had no experience in so quickly that I wouldn't even realise. I kept my distance and spoke to them in smiles instead, hoping that when they said, 'Oy, bellend, that's fucking rubbish, innit?' it wasn't about me.

December was in full throttle as I adapted to my new life and the people around me. Christmas was fast approaching, yet the only indication was the parties that I worked at and the few sprigs of holly hanging in around the pub. Nobody in the hostel really spoke about it, and I couldn't have cared less either. Working at events full of fake snow, plastic Christmas trees, and Mariah Carey songs, felt funny more than anything, especially since you'd see the Santa blind drunk five hours into the party, no matter how fancy it was.

Despite working four times a week and barely spending any money on food and drink, I was still constantly struggling. Every day, I'd apply for simple hospitality work, but with no luck. I thought working in a hostel might be nice, since I knew about the life and had London's tube map memorized by heart from the old squatting days (which I thought could be useful for the tourists). But, as usual, there were no jobs for me.

The only hopeful answer I got, and the only job interview I had, came to nothing when it turned out that they had already hired somebody the day before, and had forgotten to notify me. I had spent all my day's food money on travel that had gotten me absolutely nowhere.

I didn't even make any plans to go back to Estonia to cele-brate Christmas that year. After my mom's visit, I felt like I didn't have a reason to, like I was not worth it. I decided to sort out my life in England, instead of celebrating something I didn't have faith in and in a place that (I felt like) didn't have faith in me either.

I went to spend Christmas at Mari's – my little angel on earth's place. She was living with an English boy and a Spanish girl, so for Christmas we all compromised and had a Spanish omelette and lots of Spanish wine.

With Christmas over, so was my work at the agency. January, as I've said before, is the most depressing month of all. It's like everybody wakes up from the festive bubble, understands how they've horrifyingly wasted all their life savings on idiotic presents for people that don't even matter, have become even fatter and uglier, and are desperately trying to gain back control by working extra hard, exercising too much, and sitting at home not spending money. Of course, that all means the death of agency work – and emptiness in my wallet. Even the downstairs pub was quieter than usual, so there was nothing to do.

But I am not the type of person who can sit still. I love to work; I like to be on the go. I love reading books, learning new things, exploring what's around. In order to avoid going crazy and to keep our minds fresh, Paul and I went around the London museums. Thank God they are free – it's a true blessing.

We went to each and every free place we could, just to kill time as well as to learn something new. Fossils of rocks, plants, and animals; war memorabilia, Nazis and Jews; pregnant toads, flying butterflies;, Renaissance paintings; photographs and weird new paintings; space suits and moon landings; dinosaurs; human imperfections; medieval torture devices – we've seen them all. Many, many times.

Paul and I started to hang out so much that everybody but us took us as a couple. The truth was that we were just two youngsters from abroad, living in this big city, away from everything we knew. I guess that in each other, we found ourselves and everything that we had been missing back at home.

He taught me to play scales on the guitar (perhaps hoping that I wouldn't embarrass myself on the open mic again), and told me the reason behind the joke that all Australians are just 'English and Irish prisoners'. In my naive Estonian mind, I had never thought of racism in the way living in London kept showing me again and again.

I taught him that there are more countries in Europe than just England, Ireland, France (hot, smoking girls), Spain (crazy, sexy girls), Italy (his family was half Sicilian), Germany (Hitler), and Sweden (ABBA and hot Nordic girls). There was also places called Estonia, Finland, Latvia, Lithuania… and no, we are not Russians.

Sometimes I'd buy black bread and kefir from a Polish shop and let Paul taste the flavours of the world he never even knew existed. The bread, of course, wasn't as black and as fresh as you'd get back at home in Estonia, but it was the best you could get in London. He was happy. He ate and drank everything and loved all my stories of a country so close to his favourite girls, the Swedish. Perhaps he was hoping to get some flirting advice he could use if he ever ran into one.

After doing a little bit of research online and speaking to people around me, I decided to look for an apprenticeship. Learn while you earn, right? I applied to every opportunity in every field, not even caring what it was, just to do something. I wanted to get an apprenticeship in painting, because this was something I had done a lot and enjoyed as a child – painting my great grandma's house. She had never been proud of my foreign dance moves, but she had been proud of her newly painted walls and loved to mention them to her vodka friends. Not that they ever cared – the colour of some random house is the last thing on your mind if you haven't been sober for a week.

From that moment, my days were filled with applying for work and apprenticeships, saying yes to every opportunity and every chance, whether it was for painting or anything else.

The success rate of my apprenticeship search was as good as my job search – below zero. No phone calls, no replies, no nothing. I was like a hedgehog in the mist (an old Russian animation of a hedgehog that wanders around the misty woods, seeing some incomprehensible shit while walking around aimlessly). The animation is quite sweet, unlike the way my life was.

It showed that nobody wanted to employ me, or even teach me. Perhaps I really was that unskilled, stupid, hopeless case that could never be taught or offered anything. Maybe. Well, besides those reasons, my biggest obstacles came to be that I also:

1. Was a woman, hence the painting apprenticeship applications didn't get taken seriously,
2. Was European; not from the UK.

In proper English fashion (politically correct, as they all are), they sugar-coated all of the reasons for turning me down. And for the first month, I truly believed I could actually have a chance. They would mutter 'how cool it is for a woman to try to get into painting' yet 'how strong, even too strong for a woman, one must be'. They would all be surprised at my good English language skills, yet 'the English language skills must be one hundred per cent, one hundred per cent'. Translated into English, I should have understood that my sex and nationality just wouldn't do. But at that time, I didn't speak the language of political correctness, and I didn't recognise the words with their hidden agenda.

After struggling for weeks, I got a call from some teaching company for youngsters, inviting me to their open day. Their website promised to satisfy all my needs as a young ambitious adult wanting to educate herself, and their pictures full of smiling people with diplomas in one hand and a possible job in the other, made me hopeful. I wanted to be one of those happy people, too.

'Hello, welcome to our open day! How are you? We are great! Are you an ambitious, curious young adult, wanting to educate herself more? Then you've come to the right place! Right this way! Hello, hello, welcome to our open day…' I was greeted by this guy that looked like he was either a wind-up doll or on coke. So energised, so chatty, so joyful.

I filled out the form he gave to me and looked at him for a bit. I bet the moment this guy got home, he fell into his bed, cried into his pillow, and wanted to die out of depression. Nobody is ever that happy, unless they're hiding something horrible inside.

Another guy, who was just as smiley but less desperately chatty, took my form.

'So you're looking for an apprenticeship in painting, I see? That's very cool, usually women don't really choose that. Do you have any experience in it?' he asked me like a proper salesman.

'A little bit. I have done these—'

'So, are you employed? Darling, please fill out your employment section,' he interrupted, and shoved the papers back in my face.

'I don't have a job right now,' I replied.

'So, you are unemployed?'

'I guess so, yeah. Looking for a job right now.'

'So are you on benefits? Please tick the unemployment benefits box, thank you.'

'I am not on benefits, though I am—'

'So you are employed?'

'No.'

'So you are unemployed?'

'Yes.'

'But you are not on benefits?'

This went on for a while. He couldn't believe that I didn't have a job, nor had I registered as an unemployed. After seeing my name, he asked if I was from Poland. Romania? Bulgaria? No, no, no. He didn't know what to say when I told him I was from Estonia. His face was worried, and the rarely seen frown on his otherwise professional, perfect salesman's face grew bigger and bigger as he listened to my sad, confusing life story of unemployment and my hopes for self-education. 'What should I do? What options do I have?' I asked him.

Instead of giving me an answer, he smiled. 'Thank you for coming here. We have your phone number and we will keep in touch with you if we find anything in the painting department. Thank you so much for coming!' Then he turned around and started talking to a bunch of other people who all turned out to be youngsters with a job or their unemployment benefits boxes ticked. They had their GSCE results with them and they were ready to go. I didn't even know what a GSCE was.

I had another look around before I left in defeat. The energised bunny was still doing his spiel of welcoming everybody to this magnificent event. The other one was gathering people's filled-out forms to take them to the next level.

I left with a heavy heart and a confused mind.

I had never even thought about registering as unemployed. I liked to work and keep myself busy, so my attention was all on finding the next job. It didn't even occur to me that I could get benefits while not working. It didn't come to my mind that actually, as a European living in the UK, I was eligible to get some sort of help for my situation. I guess I was dumb, naive, and inexperienced not to know my own rights.

On the other hand, I wasn't too keen on registering anyway. All I wanted was a job or an apprenticeship, something to actually do.

The main thing seemed to be that I was too bad to be employed, but not bad enough to be made good. I was floating somewhere in the middle, in the never-neverland. But even though I had gotten nothing I wanted from the apprenticeships open day, it made me think and understand what my options really were. It was my right to claim unemployment benefits. I was eligible to get some help. And after what I had seen at the open day, I hoped they could maybe help me to get an apprenticeship somewhere. That's all I really wanted. Just a little help from my friends at the government.

After another week of failed applications, I set off to the unemployment centre.

'Where you from, my darling? Poland? Romania?' The woman behind the computer didn't even look at me. She called me 'darling' which, coming from a stranger, equals 'Hi, asshole'. Her eyes were fixed on the screen and she couldn't have cared less who was sitting across from her looking for help.

'Hello, I am from Est—'

'Bulgaria?' She was like a robot. A smart robot, by the way. She kept naming all these countries that had no association with me, nor did I really know much about them. Was she trying to show off her geography skills?

'Estonia,' I finally managed to say. I must have looked like a deer in the headlights.

She gave me a quick, surprised yet disapproving look, like the arrogant girls in your high school liked to give to the nerds. I could see her deleting whatever she had already typed in. Then she wrote Estonia, her long fake nails clicking on the keyboard one by one, letter by letter. I almost wished for a moment that I was Polish. Maybe she would like me more then and her job would be easier. All of a sudden, she stopped.

'Is that country even in the EU?' She wrinkled her brow, which was the first indication that she wasn't a robot, nor was she full of Botox. Just a bit clueless. I assured her that it was.

'So why don't you have a job? Why did you come into the UK? How long have you been here for?' She was looking at my CV, fiddling it between her fingers. I was sure she didn't want to hear my story of childhood dreams and the teenage broken heart that had brought me to this country, so I went on to tell her how for some reason nobody wanted to employ me. I told her about my idea for an apprenticeship, and what I had heard and seen at the open days.

'Hmm, darling, no, we don't do that *here*.' She loved to emphasize the word *HERE*, just to make sure that I'd know where I was. Then she lost interest in me again and fell back in love with her computer. I didn't exist anymore. Her words were confusing and her delivery was harsh.

I was about to ask about my options regarding any apprenticeships or internships, but before I could open my mouth, she handed me small documents with my name and some bars on it.

'Alright, miss, here is your sheet. Write down every place you send your CV to and the outcome into those bars. See you in a month. Thanks, bye!'

My name was misspelled and I didn't know what to do. I was used to the English not knowing how to spell my last name, and I didn't mind. I was just very confused. The place that I thought would answer my questions had just created more of them instead.

The next number was called out and another guy was already approaching the booth, staring at me to leave the chair so he could go and complain about his lack of work for the two minutes the robot woman had to share.

I looked around and saw all the other beaten-down people and their misunderstandings with the centre workers. I was one of them now. It was my present. And the hopelessness in their eyes didn't only come from being misunderstood by employers, but also from not being heard by the people who were supposed to help them in this situation.

I guess I should mention – before anybody goes crazy – that I didn't receive a single penny from the unemployment centre. As a matter of fact, I got absolutely nothing from them: no advice, no help, no money. I am not sure why. Perhaps I didn't ask the right questions? Maybe I didn't have the right documents or paperwork filled out? Maybe they really didn't want to help my sorry little immigrant ass? Who the hell knows? But I never got anything from them in any way.

Still, I spent the next two months going to the meetings once every four weeks. They ask to see your sheet with the applied jobs, question why you didn't get any of them, and then assign you the next meeting date. All my plans and the advice that I had hoped to get from those people went down the drain. Nobody seemed to care. They still miswrote my name and asked if I was from Poland, every single time.

By the third meeting, I stopped caring, too. I really didn't understand why they were trying to teach me about geography at a place like that, and what was up with their obsession with the Slavic and Balkan countries? It's very cool that they know about places like that, but what did I have to do with it? I'm from Estonia – the opposite side from these countries. It's like me going up to the English and starting to randomly talk about Spain instead – what the hell are you supposed to say to that? What the hell was I supposed to say about Romania, Bulgaria, Poland?

I needed an apprenticeship, not to be lectured on countries. Unfortunately, they '*don't do that here, love*', as they loved to say to me. They also didn't know where anybody could do it at. And they called me 'love' over and over again – another word that I understood has actually nothing to do with love or positivity. As a matter of fact, if a stranger calls you that, you better hide your stupid, worthless, unlovable face and get on with your pathetic life.

I was slowly starting to learn those little English ways. Unfortunately for me, I learned them in the harshest way possible, at a time when I was already hurt enough.

My best friend and sort-of a lover, Paul, was mostly hanging out with the girls in the bar and if I wanted to see him, I had to suck up my courage and be with them, too. I still found them terrifying. They were all witty and tough, and played pool so fiercely that I grew scared of that damn little white ball itself. They drank a lot, bantered more, and I felt like a little awkward confused dog in the midst of it all. They were too funny, too quick, too strong for me. They always had a witty answer to everything, and it was a known fact that half of the people that came to spend their time in the bar, was there solely because of the girls. The place was bumping, and you had to be tough in order to be part of it.

The whole shebang was held together and managed by the toughest woman of them all – Agata from Poland. Her hard work and strong attitude were the reason why this pub had become the most popular bar in the area in the last few years. Everything that happened in the bar, in the hostel, and in its huge garden, depended on her. During the years to come, I saw that woman only having a few odd days off here and there.

For months, I had been asking Agata for a job at the bar, although I wasn't really sure I could handle it. I had seen this place on Friday and Saturday nights: music blasting loudly, a few hundred people in the pub – fifty of them are screaming for a drink, girls running around serving many drinks and people at once, somebody running downstairs to get ice, the food lift ringing through the ear-scratching music, one of the girls running to get the food and take it to the right tables, shouting to make way. A crammed pool of people, drinks being poured, drinks being knocked over, glasses smashing, people shouting, the air filled with alcohol fumes and the steam from the dishwasher. There were only two tills, but both kept crashing due to overwork. The floor was wet from beer and spilled drinks, your shoes sticking to it. And if you weren't quick enough with the orders or didn't have a quick comeback for the challenging things customers threw at you, you were done. Complete toast. I had seen people having mental breakdowns and crying in the back room by the stairs on many occasions. Unfortunately, it was quite normal.

Even though I had asked for a job there myself, I wasn't sure if I could actually do it. Spending my weekends from 8pm-2am straight, without a break; running around like an athlete while my intellectual skills were being challenged? It wouldn't be easy. But I needed money.

Agata always said that she'd let me know when it got busier and they'd be needing more staff. *When it gets busy?* I thought to myself. *It was going to get busier than THAT?!*

To make ends meet and avoid going crazy, I started busking in central London. I had learned from Bobby that Westminster station is so big and has so many exits it is one of the only places where you don't need a licence to play. All the other stations do.

So, back to the Westminster I went, but this time to play myself. My repertoire consisted mostly of Elvis, Janis Joplin, Johnny Cash, and Rolling Stones' songs. But I made most of my money playing standard blues chords on the guitar and singing my own melodies made up on the spot. It was easy for me to pour my sad, loveless, and moneyless existence into songs, and I guess people liked it. Or did they give me money so I'd stop? Whatever their reason, the good old blues brought bread and beer on my table quite often.

Bobby was right – nobody ever bothered me while I was playing in Westminster. I could hear others playing their songs at the other exits, all of our voices echoing through the connected draughty halls. Everybody else sounded more professional, playing heaps of Adele, Amy Winehouse, and Ed Sheeran songs, with their angelic voices and great guitar skills. I was none of that. I screamed from the top of my lungs how I couldn't get no satisfaction and challenged people to take another piece of my heart, until the tips of my fingers hurt so much I couldn't touch the strings any longer and my already raspy voice had completely gone.

When it was a rainy day, I would go to Tottenham Court Road Station instead. Rain would make playing at Westminster very hard, because all the surfaces would be immediately wet and I'd have nowhere to sit. Busking standing up wasn't my thing. First of all, it's harder to play the guitar, since I didn't have the strap; and second, I felt like I was bothering people too much. On rainy days, Tottenham was the perfect place for busking. At that time, they were building and restoring the station and creating new exits, so it was easy to hide myself in one of them.

Playing at the Tottenham Court Road station was more profitable than playing at the Westminster, but it was also trickier – you never knew when you were going to get kicked out. For example, one time I had been playing for about 15 minutes when an angry homeless lady came screaming at me, 'This is my spot! You've taken my spot! I've been in the same corner for over ten years. You can't be here!' She was pointing her finger at me aggressively and it looked like she was ready to fight.

I wasn't going to argue with her. I was already impressed/ saddened enough by the fact that she had spent ten years of her life sitting in one corner, so I didn't even want to know what else she was capable of.

Another time, I sat down, got my guitar out, sang the first verse, and was immediately greeted by two undercover police-men. They took my name and address and told me I couldn't busk there. I told them my name was Linda Perry (the amazing LA producer/singer) and that my address was the local McDonalds in the corner. They knew I was lying, but they obviously didn't care. I could see that from the sweet smile one of the policeman gave me.

But if nobody kicked me out, I would play for a few hours and make about £15-25. It's not a lot of money, but busking four times a week could enable me to pay for a bed for another week, and some food while I was at it. Perhaps even a beer – oh, what a luxury!

I was busking almost daily, as often as my throat and fingers allowed me and as long as the weather wasn't too bad. I didn't do it just because of the money, but also to get away from the house and the man that I fancied – Paul. Just like Austin, he was loved by everybody in the community. Unfortunately, he had his eyes on all the English bar girls instead. So, from the early afternoon when he went down-stairs to hang out with the barmaids, I went to Westminster, sang about my gloomy life, and managed to at least make a few pounds from it.

A few weeks later, I was called downstairs to help with the Sunday food. Sundays, as every true Englishman knows, is the day of eating pub roasts and drinking hair of the dog in the same place where you got wasted just ten hours before. Now you were back with your kids, who ran around the waitresses (who were usually as hungover as you), and trying not to be sick in your plateful of pork belly and veggies. There's football on the TV screen, the pub smells of gravy, oven potatoes, and slow cooked meat, mixed with somebody's puke of last night. You know, Sundays?

And that is how I started working at the Railway. I was one of the only ones not dying of a hangover that day, so I helped the girls take food to the tables and made sure football was on in the outside area at all times to avoid the alcohol-fuelled dads from going crazy.

By the end of the evening, I was pouring drinks. Not very well, but I did it. And by the end of the shift, I was part of the bar group and laughing with them at jokes that had previously remained incomprehensible and terrifying to me.

It turned out that as soon as the doors closed and the music went soft, the girls weren't scary at all. They were really lovely. And that's how I met my new family.

14

~

From that Sunday, my life changed for ever and everything that hadn't made sense before, now did. After that day, I started working in the bar like a maniac. Days got longer and warmer which meant that the pub got more and more busy. More often than not, they were completely understaffed, and since I was usually hanging out at the upstairs hostel or in the back garden, I was always ready to jump behind the till and earn a few pounds.

I worked all the time and I was never tired. It felt like all the energy and hope I had been holding in for months while looking for a job or apprenticeship, was coming out now. I was on fire. I was on a roll. Even if I had a day off, I was hanging out by the bar, seeing what could be done. I felt unstoppable.

Within a few days, I learned what a wine spritzer was, and shandy, the measurements of strong liquors, and how to pour a Guinness. I also understood why the English get pissed so quickly when they are in Estonia – the 50ml double shot in the UK is equal to a single shot in Estonia. All the staggering, wasted English lads walking around Tallinn's cobblestones started to make more sense now.

I learned the names of the beers and ciders, wines and spirits, because my biggest fear was that with the music bumping I wouldn't understand what the 99% English clientele were saying to me and I would look like a stupid immigrant next to the gorgeous, witty English barmaids. So I figured that even if I couldn't banter with them like the other girls did, at least I wouldn't fuck up their drinks order and make them hate me completely.

The most surprising lesson I learned, though, was that the English hate when their beer has a head. They seem to think they get less than a pint, so prefer a flatter beer. I couldn't believe it. Honestly, I almost laughed when I saw the way beer was served to the rim, with hardly any bubbles in it, and people were completely satisfied with it.

I also learned a lot of English slang. For example, I came to understand that the English are obsessed with tits. 'He's off his tits, he's a tit, he just arsed over tit, I'm buzzing me tits off, tits, tits, tits.' At first, I was expecting to see some boobs, or looking for a naked lady. Confused, I soon learned that their sayings have nothing to do with women's breasts. Instead, they mean how absolutely wasted somebody is, what a moron they've become, or how excited someone is.

Another funny thing that I came to learn was asking for the toilet. English don't just say, 'Where is the loo?' or 'Where is the bathroom?' They ask, 'Where's the ladies? Where's the gents?' At first, I thought they were blind. The whole pub was full of women and men, so that's where they were!

The very first time I got asked that question, I actually answered, 'Everywhere.' The woman laughed at my reply, thinking I must have been trying to be funny. I wasn't; I was just confused. 'Oh you, I can see it now,' was her answer, as she headed off to the ladies toilet. My mind was blown! I had unlocked another English language level.

I've never made that mistake again, although I had to remind myself many times that the answer to 'Where's the ladies?' or 'Where's the gents?' is 'Around the corner', not 'Everywhere around you'.

It also came as a surprise how much the English love pubs, and do everything over a drink, whether that be tea or alcohol. Happiness or sadness, birth or wake, boredom or excitement, are all marked with a glass or a cup of the good old something, to make it better. I had always thought that eastern Europeans drank a lot but, damn, I've never seen anybody sculling down more than the English. Perhaps only the Aussies.

I couldn't keep up, although I tried. They were surprised that I was from eastern Europe but drank less than them. I didn't even have an answer to that. I was surprised at the stereotypes myself, as they were crumbling in front of my eyes.

But most of all, I learned why the girls were as tough as they were. And in order to stay in the business, I had to become one of them or get the fuck out.

I discovered in the following months that not many people could handle all the craziness that came with the bar work. Lots of people came to trial days and left less than four hours later, a bag of nerves, due to the pub being so busy and demanding. We had people who would freeze as soon as there were more than twenty people by the bar asking for a drink, or more than thirty food orders, or if there was only one functioning till for five people. But for us, the girls, moments like these meant that the party had just begun. When the newcomers ran home, shivering and stressed out about this bar work, we poured Jäegerbombs down our throats, told Tag the DJ to turn the music up so we could dance to it, and started taking orders. Bring it on! Is that all you've got?

I'm not saying it was easy. It was far from that. And the people that couldn't survive those hours weren't weak. There was one thing in common, though: you either knew how to banter and challenge the customers, or you didn't. The pretty bar girls and their skill at making drinks while making you laugh and throwing your own big words back to you, was a big part of why people came into this pub in the first place. And as I found out, it had nothing to do with how English you were.

It took me four shifts to learn all the drinks that we were selling and how to serve them properly. But it took me just one shift to understand that I wasn't going to get far with that knowledge alone.

I was completely terrified and over-analysing everything during my first few shifts, and the girls around me saved me from a few pretty awkward moments with the customers. But before I knew it, I was just as loud, feisty, and quick at both making drinks and giving comeback as I had seen from the others. I had to be to cope with comments like: 'Hey, love, can I get ya number?' 'Oy, do you need to be pretty in order to work here?' 'I'll buy you a shot if you kiss me on the cheek!' 'What time d'you finish your shift? D'ya wanna come to mine?'

You learn very soon that logic won't help you, nor will it make them understand. Bantering back is your only way out, and their only way of leaving. 'The truth is, darling, you already bought me two shots without me even having to feel your sweaty lips on my face. And by the time I finish my shift and leave this bar, you will have already been sleeping for hours. So, please, cut the shit chat and just pay for your drink, alright?'

There were times when I really didn't understand what was said to me. But when I really didn't know what to say, I'd just smile back. A sincere, genuine smile of me not comprehending their low-level cheap shot seemed to embarrass them more than me.

I have to admit that in order to survive in this chaotic, busy (yet fun) bar, we also drank. If your staff consists of a bunch of English, one Polish, Irish, Aussie, and an Estonian, you have to make room for staff drinks. These nationalities grew up on alcohol fumes and were probably made in a drunken state. So, what else do you expect from us? To be very honest, we would drink a fair bit, but never got drunk. It was so busy and there was so much running around, you ended up sweating it all out.

The ring of staff shots was sometimes all you needed. When you've been running around for the fourth hour without a break and your hands grow tired from pouring a thousandth Peroni, one strong Jäegerbomb could really make you feel alive again. Except Melissa; her sweet poison was tequila.

For a while, my days were filled with busking during the afternoons in Westminster station, and pouring pints in the evenings until 3am. I loved it. By June, I had more money than I'd had in the whole of the last year and I didn't have to worry about food or my bed space. I felt whole. I had friends both down at the bar as well as up in the hostel. There was so much going on in my life that it felt like the whole thing was an apprenticeship in itself.

Most of the girls working behind the bar had been friends since school days, and a lot of their other friends were regulars of the pub. For our regulars – our friends – the bar wasn't open from 12pm-2am; it was open from whenever we got in until whenever we left, which sometimes even meant 6am. Overall, it wasn't just a place you 'came to work' or 'came to have a quick pint'. Despite people working there three to four times a week, they'd hang out there six to seven times instead. The Railway was the place that whenever you walked in, whatever time, whatever day, you'd always find at least one of your friends there to hang out with. It was a place we liked to call 'the house that all the roads lead to', because it truly was that. Every party, meeting, get-together, happy occasion or sad moment, either started or ended there.

The amount of booze we drank and the intimate stories we told during those crazy weekend nights when five people were behind one till making ten different drinks, rubbing sweatily against each other, brought us closer and took our friendship to a whole another level. We were hanging out together outside of the bar as well, not just at work. Within a month, my social life went from knowing one Aussie guy (who finally started liking me, too) to about thirty English guys and girls.

Since the whole gang had grown up around this area, they showed me all the beauty south London could offer. 'Going to the nature' meant either visiting Brockwell Park or the lovely Crystal Palace park (where I had cried excessively a few years before and I still hated). I ate greasy chicken and chips almost every day. If I ever felt like something sweet, the girls recommended me to have a deep fried Mars bar – and loved seeing my dying face as my teeth hurt from the sugar and my arteries were becoming clogged after just one bite. They would show me their school and tell me stories of their childhood.

I also became more accustomed to the English political correctness, and started to comprehend its socialising ways. I had grown up knowing that the USA was a place where people constantly asked you friendly questions without actually caring about the answer, but I had been surprised to learn that the English did that a lot, too. 'How are you? Nice to meet you! You look lovely! What shitty weather!' is equal to 'Hello. I don't know you, nor do I care. You look weird, but whatever. The weather is always shitty, I'm just stating the obvious to kill the awkward silence I would otherwise have with you.'

I was at a moment in my life when I went out a lot and was constantly meeting new people, so I had to have a lot of these conversations. For me, it was four sentences too many. As an Estonian, a simple 'Hi, what's up?' would do. The weather is always shit, so there's no need to rub it in our faces even more.

Nor do I think that a complete stranger to me cares to hear how I am actually doing. The main thing is that we are drinking right now, and alcohol cures all wounds, doesn't it? So, I'm great! We're all frigging great!

People still considered me quiet and sweet, whereas actually I was just trying to keep up with their slang and remarks, and I smiled a lot because I didn't understand yet as quickly as I needed to. Soon enough, though – and especially after a few drinks – I also started calling people that got on my nerves 'darlings' and asked 'How are ya?' without really caring about their wellbeing.

There were, of course, still times when I slipped and was the good old, weird Estonian again, but I was never as bad as I had been when I was squatting, embarrassingly blushing in the darkness at not knowing what to say.

Well… when in Rome, act as the Romans do, innit?

Summer 2013 was sweaty and hot, and the bar was constantly packed. I remember going to work, pouring my first drink of the night, and already feeling sweat dripping down my body. That was the summer when London officially sold out of fans; it was even in the news. The Chinese couldn't work fast enough to make fans for Argos and Amazon to allow Londoners to breathe again.

That July, I went to Estonia for a week. But I couldn't wait to get out.

First of all, I had developed an accent in Estonian. Apart from the phone calls with my family every other week, there was no point in thinking, speaking, or being in Estonian, because nobody around me would have understood. Everything around me was English, from the first word to the very last thought of the day. When I got home, my sister asked if there was something wrong with me, since I spoke so slowly. My friend mocked me for sounding like a Russian imitating an Estonian, slurring my words.

I went to the beach and hung out with the Finnish grandmothers, I took walks with my dog, and saw my sisters. It was lovely, but it felt empty. My happiness wasn't there with the laughing sunbathers, and it wasn't in the woods where I took my dog. It all felt like a postcard – nice to look at, but I was living it through the eyes of someone else. My happiness lay in the rowdy bar nights, English bantering, constant police and ambulance sirens in traffic, Jäegerbombs, and roasts. Oh, I couldn't wait to be back in England!

I do remember two things, though. First, my mom mentioned how much weight I had gained, and advised me to join a gym 'or something, please!' I blame it on the fatty chips and pizzas I ate in the pub, the deep-fried Mars bars and the delicious sugary ciders with which I skulled down all these delights. In Estonia, I only ate homemade food and rarely went out, but in England the most I did in a kitchen was to boil water for my next cup of tea. Or to find a bottle opener.

The second thing I remember was the starry sky I saw for the first time in ages. It felt so weird, so beautiful, so unexpected. London's night sky was mostly cloudy, even on the clearest days, and I was too busy to look for stars while pouring drinks anyway. To see this little bit of pure nature, with the crickets in the back doing their thing, felt humbling and beautiful.

But even the stars couldn't keep me away from my true love – the crazy city with all its mad people. After spending two days in the quiet nature, I was about to go mad. I started imagining voices. I had gotten so used to different sounds and constant life around me that I didn't know how to be in silence any more.

When I returned to London a week later, and was welcomed by the good old traffic jams, sirens, and hordes of people, I felt more relaxed than I did in Estonia.

In August, Paul and I became a couple and moved together to Streatham. All these trips to the museums and late nights at the bar had brought us together, and we became very close. I was busking at the Westminster much less now, since the pain in my heart had been replaced with shared love and true happiness. And pretty rough hangovers.

Living in Streatham was the first time I started to settle down in London. Somehow, everything had magically fallen into place. I had a great job – actually, it was so enjoyable, it didn't even feel like a job. All my friends were there, breathing in and living the same vibe. And I had a great place to live, where I dared to open the two bags that I had been carrying around for over two years.

15

I was working at the pub about 3-5 times a week and getting to know the real English ways. There were all sorts of people there – young and old, laddy and posh, dickheads and sweethearts. I chatted to them all; it was part of the job. And while I was doing it, a strange thing started to occur, over and over again – people would talk to me in Polish. Here we go again. People teaching me geography and languages at very impractical places in very weird ways.

There was only one Polish word I knew when I started working at the pub – *kurwa*. Basically, whenever something goes wrong, you can apparently use that word. I learned it in the kitchen from the Polish chefs. On a busy stressful day, they would always scream '*kurwa* this, *kurwa* that!' So I learned it means fuck, shit, or something like that.

The other words/phrases are: '*Dziękuję Ci, jak się masz? Dobry.*' This means 'Thank you. How are you? Good.' These, I learned in much harder way, much later.

After some time working in the pub, I noticed some customers would look me closely, blabber some words, look at me more, go red in the face, then take their drinks and walk off. At first, I didn't think much of it. I reckoned it must be some English slang I didn't yet know, so I just smiled back to them until they left. But when it kept happening more often with different people, I began to get worried. All these z's and s's didn't sound English to me, and the other bargirls didn't seem to understand them either. So what was the problem?

I have to admit, it didn't dawn on me that they were actually trying to speak another language, and that I was expected to know it and perhaps applaud them for their efforts. I simply didn't understand why anybody would do that. Not many even know of Estonia's existence, let alone speak the language, so I certainly didn't expect to hear it. My second thought was that maybe they are having a weird mouth twitch, hence the random sounds. Maybe they were having a stroke. Should I call the doctor? Were they staring at me, trying to blink an SOS code with their eyes so that I could get help? What was happening?

I thought something was off when it kept happening more often and to nobody else but me. Was London full of mouth-twitchers who all wanted to confide in me? I finally understood what the *kurwa* was happening when Agata told me they were speaking the Polish language and that people probably considered me Polish. She translated the phrases and words I had thought were a sign of an early stroke or a speech impediment (no offence Poland). I knew I didn't look English, but in my head there were so many other places I could be from besides that one country which everybody kept throwing at my face. I started to get very worried about England's school system, particularly its geography teaching.

Even though Agata was the only Polish woman in our group, she wasn't ever spoken to in Polish, unlike me. And she made sure it stayed that way. Whenever somebody mentioned something about eastern Europe somewhere, she smiled, made a witty joke that shut everybody up, and left. She had been in London for over ten years and never spoke about her Polish heritage, the language, nor the country. Yes, she did have a slight accent, but she made sure never to get into the discussion about its origin. I never understood why.

I loved talking about Estonia (that got constantly mixed up with Australia) and seeing people's surprised faces, as they had no idea about my country. Unfortunately, the conversations were always cut short because there was not much to say. As soon as people understood I didn't speak Polish or Russian and that we weren't a village in Poland or Russia, they went quiet and left. It was such a shame. I had so much to say, yet nobody cared to listen.

Once again, I started to wish I was Polish, just as I had in the jobcentre. Perhaps then people would know what was going on and would talk to me more. Then they could say *Kurwa dobze*! and we could both laugh at this beautiful life. Then every official place that had to know my nationality would get it right the first time, without having to ask me additional questions. Oh, I really did start wishing I was Polish.

Knowing these four words changed my whole world. From that day on, I didn't have to worry about the health of London's men, because I now understood that they had just tried to speak to me in my own supposed mother tongue. From that day on, I could at least tell the guys, 'Good on ya, lads, for knowing another language, but I'm not Polish. You're welcome for your drinks though, enjoy!'

You'd think that would be the end of the conversation. That they'd say, 'Alright, fair enough, I'm gonna go get pissed with my mates now.' But to my surprise, for some reason people liked to put their hands up as if they had been just arrested, then give me an innocent, frightened look. 'Hey, I didn't say anything,' they'd say defensively, trying to make sure they were cool and not racist.

'Where you from then?' they'd ask hastily, just to kill what had become an awkward silence.

'Estonia.'

Now, this could then go one of two ways.

1. His face would lighten up and he tried to imitate the accent from the land down under: 'Oh, Australia! Ah yeah, how's the beaches and the kangaroos, eh? You finally free from the clink, eh?'

Very funny. Having lived very closely with Aussies for a year by that point, I knew how much they love the kangaroo jokes. Or being called ex-convicts. I cringed inside for them as the people in front of me thought they were the best jokers in the world, laughing at their own original discovery. It got cut short, though, when I told them I couldn't come from a more opposite place, and repeated it was Estonia.

'Huh. Do you have kangaroos there?'

'No, we have polar bears.' Just like Aussies use the kangaroo jokes to get away from a stupid conversation, every Estonian uses the polar bear one. It shuts people up because nobody wants to go to a country where you freeze your tits off and get eaten by a bear, so it works like a mosquito repellent.

'Oh...' They'd then take their drinks, leave, and make sure they got served by another bartender for the rest of the night, which was fine by me.

2. 'Hmmm... Essstooniiaa...' They'd look at me weirdly, thinking I might have a mouth twitch or a stroke, blabbing words they'd never heard of. To kill the awkward silence and to have a chance of talking about my home, I'd ask them if they knew where it was.

'Yeah, yeah, it's in... it's where Romania and Bulgaria are, innit? All those... you know, Romania and them...' Damn. What was it with those three countries that everybody loved to shove in my face? Also, wrong direction again. Just a little note: not every country that ends in the same syllables lies in the same spot.

Occasionally, of course, I would run into somebody who knew the existence of my little country and perhaps had even been there. They always asked me what I was doing in London when I could spend my days in untouched nature and a cool, spacious town instead. 'Tallinn is gonna be the next best thing in Europe, London's time is over. What are you doing here?' was always their question, accompanied by a confused, worried face. 'I will go back one day,' I'd tell them, not wanting to get into the details about how much I loved London's craziness and tried to avoid the nature and the life Estonia had to offer me. They would never understand. They always gave me sad look as they left with their drinks.

Either way, I seemed to be the bad guy in all three scenarios. Can you see now why I started to wish I was Polish? I could have avoided all three awkward scenarios if I was, and would have had to explain myself less, if even at all.

But truth be told, I was not one bit sad. I was having the time of my life.

Soon enough, it was my third Christmas in England, and I finally got to see the real English one. I was working on the 24th of December, expecting it to be quiet and holy; it was Jesus' birthday, after all. But I was in for a surprise. The English love to celebrate it with a bang. We were having a proper knees-up, except that we were wearing Santa hats and getting drunk on mulled wine and mulled cider, instead of our usual beer and vodka cocktails. We had a steel drum band playing Christmas carols, while everybody in the pub was having roasts and singing along with their families. We even had

Glitterbombs instead of our usual Jäegers, just to spice up the occasion. Everybody was feeling festive and lovely. It was like a Saturday night's sweet rowdiness mixed with Sunday family roasts. It was so beautiful.

The tables were full of mince pies, pigs in blankets, and Christmas puddings. I had always loved mince pies – the supermarket bins are full of these sweet Christmassy delights from the end of December to mid-January, and during squatting time, we stuffed our faces with them for weeks.

This year, I tried Christmas pudding for the first time in my life – and probably the last. It is one of the most horrible things I've put in my mouth, and I don't even know why. Alcohol? Check! Dried fruits? Yes, please! Spices? Lovely! But to put all these ingredients together like that? I almost puked. I'll stick to mince pies instead.

I did think about my family, though. I was pouring drinks and singing along to 'On the fifth day of Christmas my true love sent to me…' while they were probably eating potatoes, blood sausage, and sauerkraut, and watching silly festive shows. They had become used to me not being at home for Christmas, and so was I. We exchanged our greetings during the daytime via phone, but that was it. It didn't feel like there was anything else to say.

The next day, on the 25th, we went to Agata's. Her boyfriend had cooked 12 Christmas foods – apparently, it's some sort of a huge tradition thing in Poland, and represents the 12 Apostles. Now, you'd think that all eastern Europe is the same with its traditions, yet I had never heard of some twelve Christmas Apostles along with all its Jesus talk. In Estonia, we are too occupied with learning poems, turning neighbours into Santa Claus, and talking to the old spirits, that nobody really has time to check the Bible. Nevertheless, I was more than happy to eat the Polish outcome. He had cooked turkey and borsh, bread, different salads, pies, and potatoes, all to be washed down with many vodka shots. It was amazing. That Christmas was truly beautiful and, if I do say so myself, a pretty wonderful time of the year.

It was 2014 and life was great. In January, I went to Estonia for a week again, and this time Paul came with me. It was quite funny, actually. This Aussie boy really didn't know what winter was before coming to Estonia. Within the first few hours of being in the country, his trainers became unusable due to endless amounts of snow and the freezing temperature.

We went to the countryside, where he almost pissed himself seeing the traces of wolves and lynxes, hearing how they might come out any time, and if you don't know how to act, you might end up as their dinner. My sisters and I went to the beach (completely iced-over and white, with no horizon or trees in sight) and asked him to take us back home. He started walking towards Sweden. If he'd kept on walking, he would have gotten there in a few days… or died on the way. It was funny, because all the rules of nature that I had learned as a child and hence found logical, were all so new and strange to this city boy. We went to the medieval Tallinn, where he ate elk soup and drank so much beer I didn't think they would let him on the plane.

Once back in London, he asked me why I chose to stay in England when there was so much happening in Estonia, especially in Tallinn. But I told him to shut up and go back to Australia if he wanted to talk about it again. Nothing, and I repeat nothing, was gonna come between me and the city I loved – London.

My life was spent at the Railway or around it. All of us friends, co-workers, the regulars, and the acquaintances from around, worked and partied as one. Seasons changed and as the new spring arrived, we got more staff to join our lovely family. We had another crazy summer with all its steamy windows, shots, and dancing. Me and Agata weren't the only foreigners behind the bar any more, either. Laura joined us from Spain, and when that girl started dancing, everybody was watching. When she said, *'Hola, que tal?'* everybody screamed in sync: *'Hola, muy bien!'* And there'd be more shots, more dancing, more singing.

I imagined myself saying in Estonian *'Tere, kuidas läheb?'* (*"Hi, how are you?"*) to the same people she did. But the answer would be silence. An awkward, weird silence, accompanied by muttering about what was wrong with this girl. It's different with English, Spanish, Italian, and French. Everybody can say *Ciao bella, Bonjour mademoiselle, Hola mi amor*. Ah, it must be great to come from a big country that everybody knows about and people can say a few words in your language. I guess I will never know that feeling, but there's nothing I can do about it. Nor would I want to, come to think about it.

After the sweaty summer came autumn and winter again. Once the winter arrived, it was time for me to leave the pub. After two years of working there, I decided to quit the pub. New winds were blowing through all of our lives, and everybody was longing for a change, finding new jobs outside of bar work. I was done with working until 3am and all the craziness Railway had to offer me, and I simply couldn't imagine myself doing it any longer.

I decided to join an agency again, remembering how easy the job had been – that is, if you can wear that ridiculous penguin suit. But I needed a simple, easy job. My life as a bargirl at the Railway was finished, as it was for a lot of my friends. But it remained our favourite spot, and it still is – a place that all roads lead to. Every party, every get-together, every celebration, either starts or ends there. This house, this hostel, and the people in it, are the reason why I stayed in England. And damn, do I love it.

The beginning of 2015 was full of new opportunities and life-changes for all of our group. Paul and I moved to our own little flat in Upper Norwood, that cost us only £825 per month plus bills. For the two of us having our own place in London, that was a real bargain! He started working at the Ritzy cinema in Brixton (along with a lot of our other Railway friends) and I joined an events agency as waiting staff. The job wasn't brilliant, but it enabled me to see all the great historical places in London while doing easy work. And after working such long and crazy shifts at the Railway, it felt like God's gift.

Getting our own place was a very grown-up thing to do. After all, we were two mature, settled adults now. Or so we both wanted to think.

Until then, every place I'd ever rented had included the bills in the price, so I had never really thought of what must be paid and how much. Now it was my turn to find out all the lovely bills the English government charged. Besides the obvious water and electricity, there were a few that I couldn't help but laugh and cry about at the same time:

1. TV licence! That doesn't even include the channels themselves. It's just for owning that damn box. Fortunately, we didn't have a TV, and even though the contract forced us to pay the fee, we did not. We got calls from them every other month asking what channels we watched, and they sounded quite upset when I said we watched nothing so we'd pay nothing.

2. Council tax. Oh, the most evil and expensive of them all. Apparently, this tax was implemented so we could have cleaner streets and good infrastructure, neither of which

I encountered in Norwood. I lived near Crown Point, which looks like a dump itself. Every day after 3pm when the kids got out of school, the place was full of empty chip boxes covered in burger sauce and half-eaten chicken wings, all thrown onto the ground. Bins were overflowing, and there were beer cans in corners. It reminded me of my childhood in the 90s when there were syringes, alcohol bottles, and food packets lying around everywhere in Estonia. But this was London, the supposedly beautiful western Europe, the land of the royals, in the 2010s. Estonia's streets got cleaned up as the 90s ended. Unfortunately, I don't have enough money to pay to get London's streets clean, too.

Perhaps the infrastructure, the transport, is better? Not really. My stop was on top of a slight hill, so the bus had to make extra effort to get up there to go towards Crystal Palace, which is even hillier. Here comes my question: have you ever sat in a burning bus? I have, multiple times. Yes, you can smell the fire. Yes, you can see the black smoke through the windows, bursting out from the back. But you only have two stops left until your home and you've spent half an hour waiting for this bus to come in the first place, so you stay on it.

You only move once the other passengers or the bus driver start screaming for their lives and the bus can't go any further without exploding. Then you take your exhausted ass and walk up the hill until you're home. You paid for the bus ticket and you pay shitloads for the council tax so that the transport will work and you can get home. But, unfortunately, you don't really get to taste the benefits of this council tax if you live in Upper Norwood. Or maybe this is the good life? Who knows how bad it would be otherwise? I don't want to know.

It took about two months for our excitement about a happy mature life to turn into a messy existence where both supposed adults were constantly confused and out of money due to all the bills. Even the rent that we had considered so cheap at first turned out to be too much once we found out everybody else living in that house was on benefits, had gotten their homes from the council, or didn't have to pay a penny.

Also, we didn't really live alone. Certainly, nobody told us off if we didn't clean the dishes immediately after eating, but the thinner-than-paper walls that every London house seems to be made of ensured we heard and smelled everything our neighbours did, ate, and said.

There was an older English couple living upstairs from us, who stayed home all day watching silly talk shows on the telly and smoking cigarettes out of their window. The few ornaments we had on the table would tremble at night due to the snoring from above. Opposite us lived a young, hippie English woman who had adopted all the five cats she had seen lurking around the streets. I would see her every day walking around in her PJs with a cup of tea, talking to her animal friends as they all ran away from her. She would have had a field day if she had lived in Estonia, since there are as many stray cats wandering around there as London has foxes. Next to us lived a single mom with her newborn baby and her mother, but they were always so angry that I didn't even dare to speak to them.

I think the only person who I saw and who wasn't on benefits was the Jamaican on the top floor. When he wasn't working, he'd blast reggae out of his windows for hours, just to piss off the elderly couple living in the middle of us. So, our ground floor flat was constantly full of the sounds of crappy English talk shows, reggae music, growling cats, and proper trumpet snoring at night. And if I left the house, I had to have a thirty-minute chat about cats – their food, their hair, and their lifestyle with a stoner. Did I already mention I was more of a dog person? Because I definitely am.

As usual, Paul became friends with them all, as he does with everybody everywhere. The next Christmas, when we received holiday cards from our dear neighbours, they were all addressed to Paul, none for me. Even the angry mama next door wished him happy holidays. What can I say? There's only so much I can talk about cats, babies, and snoring until I give up, whereas Paul could go on forever on every subject.

And in the winter time, when I had been working for the agency for almost a year and my self-esteem had gotten lower than I'd ever thought it could, the last thing I wanted to do was talk to more people.

16

Having worked for an agency before, I already knew what to expect – which is nothing. The less you speak, think, and are, the better for everybody. All these events are organised to the smallest detail, and the waiting staff play such an insignificant role, that the less effort you put in the more likely you will get hired (even though they try to say otherwise). However, I am better than that, and working at the Railway had given me enough experience and courage to do almost any job, but its intensity had also sucked me dry to the point I wanted something easy, a place where I didn't have to think. And agency work is perfect for that. Also, they always need people. The biggest obstacle was whether I wanted to wear that awful suit and make myself look like a penguin again.

So, what is agency work? Basically, it's as simple as A, B, C. Every time some rich fella wants to throw a party for something somewhere, they call the agency, and waiting staff rocks up to make it happen. Whatever the people, whatever the party, as long as you've got money, they'll be there. Well, truth be told, they pay shitloads for their event to happen, but the workers there are on a zero-hour contract, don't get holiday pay or sick leave, and earn about £7-8/ph. The job is very flexible, making it perfect for students and people who will never get paid for what they actually do, aka artists. Unfortunately it's also flexible on the employer's side. There have been occasions when I've waited for the bus to go to work, all ready in my penguin costume, only to find out that the shift has been cancelled. So it goes two ways. Neither of them is ideal.

Getting agency work is also very simple. You really have to be a knobhead not to get it. All you have to do is show up and not be horrible. You don't even need any special skills. What you need is to bring your own clothes, and Primark is perfect for this. Get a white and black men's shirt, even if you're a petite woman. Add the black trousers, which are not that bad, but the policy demands them to be, again, big enough to give you a flat butt. Shoes have to plain black, preferably leather, so Shoezone became my go-to place for this horrendous footwear. If they looked remotely nice, they had to be switched and waxed till you could see your own reflection and your dark future on those black shoes.

The worst thing was hair. If you were a girl who had longer hair, you had to squeeze it all into a bun, comb every little bit on your head back tight and drown it in gel, so that it worked like a natural Botox for your face. Due to that, we all suffered from bad headaches, as everything had to be so tight that it stopped all the blood flow to the head. In some ways, that was kinda good, because you didn't really have to think during working.

Men had to be clean shaven. Short-haired girls had to use anything they could to hide what they had. Basically, you could be the most beautiful person in the world, but after going through the agency makeover, nobody would be able to even tell your sex. Women look exactly like men, with their hair pulled back and baggy penguin clothes, so you all melt into one big blob of something that serves the rich fellas food and drinks and talks as little as possible. Make-up wasn't allowed, and the only jewellery you could wear was your wedding ring. After some time, even the single people became 'married', just so they could keep a piece of themselves with them.

Your job tasks depend on what you do. At dinners, you are given your own table to keep an eye on and make sure they have water, bread, and wine at all times. If you are not running to the kitchen getting them food, you stand there making sure they have everything they need and can quietly listen to their fancy stories. This was actually quite funny and enjoyable, because it differed from my own life so much.

You meet celebrities and other famous people mostly when you work at the stadiums and arenas. I ended up working in the boxes, which means somebody has paid shitloads of money to see the fiasco closely, and all I had to do was serve them food and drinks while being able to be part of it, too. Also, working in boxes is the only time in this job that you are encouraged to talk (even too much) and be as fun as possible. That way, you might even get tipped at the end of the day. Of course, that only happens if the box belongs to 'normal' people, the ones that actually had to pay for those seats and appreciate every minute of it because they've been in the bad seats for too long. They are the nicest.

One time I got £120 in tips. To this day, I can't really believe it myself. But frankly, I worked damn hard for it. I bantered eight hours in a row with five old men from Liverpool who hated the fact that their usual waitress Claire wasn't there. 'Why don't the Polish stay in their own country instead of coming here?' I heard them mutter to each other while I was opening their beers, my hands shaking, and with a lump in my throat.

In order to get through the day without crying, I had to gather up all the bantering skills I had learned while working at the pub and sharing a room with ten Aussies. Initially, they challenged my accent and commented on how 'Claire did things differently; she knew the correct English ways'. But after some time, they were impressed I even spoke English and knew a thing or two about football. They gave me a big tip because I had challenged their Liverpool accents and 'correct ways' back to them, which they found hilarious. Then, they even mentioned how much they liked Estonia and what great stories they had heard about my country.

But that's the thing with the English – they love to banter. If you can banter back, you're good to go; no matter what country you're from or what you look like, you're in. But if bantering is really not your thing and you can't keep up with the witty remarks and compliments that sound like insults (or vice versa), then it's better to get out of this country while you still have some self-esteem left. Otherwise, they will destroy you sooner or later.

I did cry later once my shift was over that night, but nobody ever saw me. And that is all that matters.

I am sure that the organisers working at those events would disagree, but my experience with this work is that nobody cares if you are doing the best job or the worst job. *Nobody cares*. At first, I was super-active and helpful, because that is what I'd had to be at the Railway. Now, I was getting told off for thinking and doing too much. So I stopped. In order to keep my job, I did less of it.

I became damn good at this job. The Railway had taught me how to be efficient and fast at the same time, so I was good. I was *damn* good. My hair and shoes might not have been up to standard at all times, but my service was. Always.

My good service even took me to Buckingham Palace garden parties. Each spring, the royal family hosts five parties to honour different people who have done something great that year. Sometimes, members of the royal family are there themselves. I did two parties: one was for aristocrats; the other for the so-called 'normal but amazing' people.

Yes, I met the Queen. Big stuff, you'd think. But it wasn't really. For me, it just meant giving my already gel-sprayed, hardly-breathing hair an additional can of that substance, getting complaints about why I had bird shit under my immaculate-looking shoes (we all did), lying that I didn't have any digestion problems (we all did from those sandwiches we were forced to eat), and being told about hundred times the main rules of meeting the Queen: do not speak unless spoken to, and don't make any sudden movements. They kept repeating it, although frankly we waiting staff were too hungry and tired to move or to even speak to each other, let alone to an old woman who couldn't care less about us anyway.

Stay humble, stay polite, show your best demeanour. Before the party began, about one hundred of us were all made to stand in the garden in one big row, in our white shirts and black pants, hands behind us, hair so glued to your scalp nobody could tell who you were, while she walked past us. This was her way of thanking us for working at her party, they said. I thought she was alright, but I would have preferred her thank you to be 'Hey, have some food before your shift, and sit down. There's nothing happening for hours.' That would have helped us all a lot more and been much more relevant to reality. But, what can you do? Life is what it is.

Once those five minutes are over, you can return to the burning sun and learn by heart the names of sandwiches that you're serving at the party, over and over again. Mint and cucumber on a white buttered bread, ham and French mustard on wholemeal.

Oh, you might wonder why I had bird shit under my shoes in the first place. Well, we all had that there. The truth is that Buckingham Palace Gardens (the bit where the workers hang out, not the fancy bit) is full of geese and other birds flapping about, and they shit everywhere. There was so much of it that it was hard to walk, and no matter how much you tried to avoid it, some of it did get under your shoes. I could smell it while we were serving aristocrats their afternoon tea with cakes and sandwiches. '*Bon appetit*, my dear rich friend.' These walls are up there for many reasons.

I have to add, though, they do have workers walking around with a vacuum-style thingy to suck all that crap up. But I guess the birds are just too fast.

You might ask why I stayed in this job for so long when it was so obviously brain-numbing and taught me nothing except rich table manners. Well, to be honest, I did enjoy being part of these fancy parties and dinners. Even though the rent at Upper Norwood was cheap(ish), the bills and expensive transport made sure that no matter how much I worked, I was always living from pay check to pay check, without a penny for anything in between. I was so broke and tired in my real life that it was great to feel part of something so different to my reality. When the 1% spoke, I did listen – even if it was just for laughs.

Working there was an escape from my own bullshit, and being part of a life I wish I could live one day, too. And I have to admit, I loved being assigned a table and taking care of the people around it. I was responsible for something, at least. I had control over something, at least. Bread, wine, water. Water, wine, bread. As long as I had those three things with me, my table was having fun – and so did I, through the jokes and the silly little problems that rich people have.

'Oh dear, I'm starting to feel guilty, I haven't been to the meetings in a month! There's just so much to do. This weekend I'm in London, then New York, then Berlin! Oh, I feel so guilty!' she gasps in despair to the older man next to her, trying not to spill her glass of Pinot Noir.

'Oh, that's nothing! I once didn't go there for half a year and nobody said anything! What could I do? It was a very nice summer in the Caribbean that year,' he answers, banishing all her worries. Then they'd laugh and ask for a refill, so they could toast the good life.

I imagined being in the Caribbean as well. Looking at them made me feel intoxicated and happy, just like they were, even though I hadn't had a single sip. A few hours later, I would be out in the streets, taking the last tube to Brixton, then waiting for ages in the cold rain for the number 196 to arrive, hoping this bus wouldn't catch fire before my home stop. And once I did get home, I would be welcomed by the snores of the upper neighbours and the cats and foxes growling outside.

I much preferred to fill up their glasses and listen to their beautiful stories of faraway lands of no problems. I did enjoy those dinners, very much indeed.

By the end of the year, I had worked at the most prestigious, over-the-top, gorgeous parties you can ever imagine. If the summer events had been like something out of a movie, then Christmastime was when the filthy rich people made sure everybody would know how well off they really were. There was so much turkey and cranberry sauce at each event that even the waiting staff got to have a taste of this amazing food. It was Christmas indeed, even for the poor! My tastebuds were happy and my digestive system even more.

Outside of the fancy parties, my own Christmas, however, was sad. Most of my and Paul's money went on bills and the constantly delayed London Transport, so we bought no gifts and made no special food.

All these frustrations regarding our money situation, crazy neighbours, burning buses, and anxiety, started to affect our relationship as well. We were both in a dark place, in a deep, black, depressing hole, and instead of working together, we turned against each other. My sadness just made him angry. His anger made me even more sad. It was a vicious circle we didn't seem able to get out of, no matter how we tried.

Along with the constant lack of money and ever-growing bills, I grew so anxious and felt so trapped in my life that I didn't know what to do. We argued more than we made love. And then we would argue about arguing, too. Our third anniversary was spent fighting while listening to *Gloomy Sunday* on repeat, and I felt exactly like the lyrics said.

I stayed at this agency work because I wanted to get a taste of a good life and this job enabled me to dip my feet into it, to smell the forbidden fruit. I didn't, of course, agree with everything that I heard was said or done, but it was fun. My reality felt dark and my work life was a splash of light in between.

Sadly, I should have known better. It was the beginning of 2016. To my ignorance, I have to admit, I never really read the news much. Besides knowing a few names and bigger happenings, I have never cared for politics. My own life was dark and sad enough, so I couldn't take in more horrors of the world, too.

But I guess I should have. If I had, I would have been more prepared for what was about to come. I would have been less surprised, naïve, and hurt. Because there are some things that you can't even mend with good old bantering or alcohol.

Brexit was coming.

17

~

2016 started off well, even hopeful for me. Besides the crippling anxiety that was constantly inside me, my love life a shambles, and my bank statement making me happy if I had even £30 after paying bills, I still felt hopeful. 2016 was going to be my time; the year when I finally took a leap of faith and changed my life around.

After spending countless hours in the back kitchens with students, discussing different topics and ways of life, I decided to enrol in university myself. I needed to step up on the ladder of my life somehow, and thought going back to school could be the answer.

I chose journalism, because I've always loved writing and am curious about everything that is going on in the world. I don't really like talking to people, but living in England for over four years had at least made me good at faking it. So I figured if you put all these three things together – writing, talking, and being curious – you get a journalist.

The university I wanted to get into the most was UAL – University of Arts, in Elephant and Castle. In order for me to be selected for an interview, I had to write an essay on a recent article that had affected me the most.

I didn't read many newspapers, or news for that matter, so the only info I got was through word of mouth or on my Facebook wall. Sometimes, if I had a long way to travel to work, I would flick through the *Evening Standard* to kill time.

And one evening I had read the investigative story of Angell Town – the other side of Brixton – where crime and poverty are London's highest. It was a story by David Cohen, and in the upcoming weeks, I read every article he wrote on the subject.

I had no experience of living the life that the people in his articles did, although we all walked the same streets, went to the same shops, hung out in the same places. Their lives differed from mine like day does from night. This journalist had spent a week in Brixton, hanging out with the gangs and the communities to understand what was going on and why.

I wrote about this article because, for me, Brixton is home. And the so-called 'bad guys' weren't bad guys at all, once you spoke to them. They were just different. Unfortunately, in this world, being different means being bad, unsuitable, and unacceptable a lot of the time. I wrote about the inequality and the misunderstandings that a simple thing like skin colour or appearance can do to a person's life.

I was on cloud nine when I received the invitation for an interview. I was so nervous, I was afraid I wouldn't manage get a single, comprehensible sentence out of my mouth, and I was ready to pass out the whole time I was there. But a few weeks later, when I was counting pennies to top up my Oyster to get to work, I received an email saying I had been accepted to UAL. I cried out of happiness, to the point that I was almost late for work.

That evening, I didn't mind the managers screaming at me, or my hungry belly, or the fact that I had a headache from how tight my hair was tied together. I felt invincible. I had finally found the light in my long, dark, miserable life. In September, I was going to be a student at the UAL. In September, I was going to be happy.

Still, even though I had been accepted to uni, I had to do few things before I was fully enrolled. For example, I had to take an English language test to show my proficiency and the level I was at. I also had to prove my residency, and apply early for a student loan so that all my documents could be processed by September when the course started. Oh boy, was I excited! I got all the document process rolling the next day, leaving me six months to get everything sorted.

It was spring 2016 and I was working for the agency and enjoying the beautiful side of life through the fancy events and even fancier guests. In the next half a year, I was going to become a student myself, studying in one of the biggest arts universities in the world. I was hopeful about my future; I was happy about my life. During the day, I was making sure that all my papers were correctly sent to the student loan company, and I read more papers to keep myself up-to-date with my new life; in the evenings, I listened to the beautiful stories of the rich people so that I could forget my own reality.

Brexit was already all over the news. Immigrants this, immigrants that. Boris Johnson and Nigel Farage say this, David Cameron says that. Poland this, Romania and Bulgaria that. The English really are obsessed with those three countries, aren't they? Well, good for them. Knowing geography is a useful tool. 23rd of June was going to be the referendum day. 23rd of June is Jaanipäev in Estonia, Midsummer's Day, and I decided to go and celebrate it there that year.

I think it was in early April when the events changed. When I would do my usual service of bread, water, and wine, the people around my table wouldn't want to talk to me any more. I could ask them the usual questions of which wine or bread they would prefer, but they would just hum and turn their heads away, instead of answering me. I had to start guessing what they wanted, and if they wanted anything at all.

There were whispers around the table as I was serving food, filling their glasses, offering bread. Whereas before, people had treated me politely like a waitress, now I started to feel like an invisible, annoying, little thing. There would be nice, friendly chatter around the table but it stopped as soon as I got there. If anybody did look at me, it was as if they were examining my appearance and work skills, their quizzical faces mixed with confusion and disgust.

I know I didn't look my best in this penguin suit from Primark and my Sonic the Hedgehog hairdo. But their looks held something more than that, as if they wanted to say something but couldn't. Maybe they felt bad for me? I did, too. Don't worry, sir, I'll keep the wine flowing for ya and you oughta not worry about me or my headache at all.

But I wasn't the only one that was struggling with my table. This gorgeous girl from Romania was also stuck with a table of deaf chatters who ignored her every question and only spoke to each other. So did the Italian boy to my left. Maybe it was just a bad night? We all have them. But at least the Canadian girl seemed to be having fun with her tablemates, and the English guys in the middle were joking while pouring wine to the guests at their table. They all seemed to have a jolly good time.

This scenario started to occur more and more, almost at every event. People spoke to me less and less, no matter what I asked, no matter how nicely. They looked at me more, examining my every move, trying to find out something but I couldn't figure out what. I could no longer escape into their beautiful stories of faraway lands and small problems, because they rarely spoke around me. Instead, they waited patiently for me to leave the table so they could mutter something to each other. It started happening to my other colleagues more, too. The more I smiled, the colder they were; the more I asked, the less they spoke, no matter how many glasses of wine they all drank.

I was working at a beautiful dinner on a lovely spring evening when I started to understand what was actually going on. My table of ten sophisticated, classy-looking people were in a good mood, chatting to each other, complimenting the decor of the hall and the flower bouquets in the middle of the tables… Until I opened my mouth to ask them whether they would like red or white wine, still or sparkling water. Then the smiles vanished, and their chats became quiet mutters as they examined my pouring skills and looks. I had gotten used to it, unfortunately. In the last month I had encountered that sort of behaviour at almost at every dinner table I'd served.

The only people loud enough were three slightly older gentlemen, their immaculate suits barely covering their huge bellies, their voices so clear and strong you could tell giving speeches and influencing people were part of their profession.

After they had finished their *entree* and I went to fill up their glasses again, I heard things that had never been said to my face before, although I'm sure they had been thought.

'It's a load of bollocks, that EU! Just look at the waitresses here. They're clearly not English; all bloody immigrants milking our rich economy. I wonder if any of them could even speak English? You think any of them could actually hold a conversation besides talking about bread and wine? Do you think?' said the guy in the middle – the youngest of them all – just as I was pouring him a glass of wine which he emptied almost instantly after his great speech. Half of the table laughed. The other half looked at me, annoyed, wondering when I would be finished serving so they, too, could say something. I kept going, not really sure if what I was hearing was correct.

'Yeah, well, that's why we are having the vote this summer, my dear," said another with a slight smirk on his face.

'Well, it's just that... they really don't fit in here now, do they? I don't mind the foreigners, but they just don't fit in here. Look what London has become – *Polish* are everywhere!' I heard this lovely lady say in a quiet voice to the big guys, whispering the word Polish and giving me a slight look, worried that I might hear her talking about my home country. The guys, though, couldn't have cared less. They'd had plenty of wine and had plenty of wisdom regarding the UK, EU, and everything in between, and they weren't afraid to declare it to the world.

'Or Czechs; they have started coming here massively as well,' said the third man – the quietest of the three – as he was carelessly biting into his bread.

'Ah, Polish, Czechs, who cares? They're all the same bloody poor, ex-USSR countries! That's why they come here. Their own countries are so shit and make so little money, it's fucking bollocks down there; they need us, they want what we have!' the loudest one told everybody.

They all laughed, nodded, and toasted proudly with the glasses I had just filled up for them. Me, the citizen of an ex-USSR country. Me, the supposed miserable, poor, non-English speaking imbecile who was milking this rich country out of its goodness.

They raised the glasses again, this time toasting 'Let's hope that people vote right this summer, shall we?' as I was slowly walking away, baffled, to go to the kitchen and collect their main courses.

For the rest of the evening, I didn't know what to say. I didn't even dare to ask them if and what beverage they would like. Were they saying these things in front of me on purpose? If so, why? They had obviously heard my accent when I first spoke to them, and I couldn't figure out whether they deliberately wanted to hurt me with these words or if they didn't really think I would understand them. I will never know, because I never dared to ask.

I knew that any sort of misunderstanding with the client could result in me losing my job and, honestly, paying rent and not drowning in bills was my first priority. So I stayed quiet. Anyway, I was too baffled and speechless that I would probably have proved them right with my non-perfect English skills. But every time the waiting staff returned to the kitchen, you could see the difference between the 'immigrants' and the 'non-immigrants' simply by asking how their night was going.

'They're alright. This guy on the right is pretty fit,' would be the normal answer from an English girl.

'They refuse to speak to me and are giving me the weird eye,' would be the answer of anybody who had an accent.

Event by an event, day after day, week to week, it went on. The only place we were all considered to be the same was in the back of a dirty, busy kitchen. Out front, there was a clear distinction of 'us' and 'them'. The ones with an accent and the ones without. The wanted and the unwanted.

These dinners, along with these conversations, became normal the more time went on. Serving champagne and canapes at garden parties and launches, or wine and mains at a dinner, I would continually hear people in suits discussing the failures of the EU and the immigrants who were to blame for everything in this country.

'They don't speak proper English, they've taken our jobs, they don't fit in!' It sounded like what Hitler used to say about Jews: they've taken your jobs, they are taking over Germany, they are the reason why you are poor and unemployed. Jews, jews, jews! Immigrants, immigrants, immigrants!

It was funny that they used the word 'immigrants' – aka people from all over the world that have come to stay in one country – when my experience says something else. You see, it's funny because there was a difference depending on where you came from. A huge, huge difference.

First of all, the French. The French accent is considered sweet and sexy all around the world. Everybody knows their country is beautiful and their cuisine is divine. As a matter of fact, probably half of today's menus are written in French and offer the best quality food from there. A quarter of the world speaks this gorgeous language, and the other three-quarters wish they could. Pass!

Scandinavia is lovely. Beautiful, blonde women, never-ending winter, ABBA, IKEA, great education, and they all speak perfect English. They pass the quality test, too.

America, Canada, and Australia are in a class of their own. The fact that these nations are here usually means that they are students, hence they are smart and cool. They are doing this waitressing job just for fun, not for necessity, and to get some extra pocket money. You can talk to them about anything and they will understand; they all speak English, after all, even though their accents might be a bit funny. Still, pass!

Every Englishman knows that Spanish beaches and wines are hard to beat, and Ryanair flies there many times a day for a very cheap price. Everybody can mumble something back in its language, even it' complete gibberish. Spain is cool. Spain is like a retirement home for the English, where you buy a house in Marbella or Mallorca and can spend your leftover years tanning on the beach and drinking Estrellas. Also, if they closed down the Spanish borders, where would they film *Love*

Island? Everybody loves *Love Island*! Oh, the tragedy! Pass! Spain must pass!

With Spain, you also have half of Latin America under your belt. The other half is Portuguese, and there are heaps of them in England. Unfortunately, even though Portugal and its friends in South America produce great wines, amazing food, and also have fantastic beaches, it still isn't as cool as its neighbour, Spanish. Pass, I guess… almost.

Then there's the English themselves. It doesn't really matter if they have African/Caribbean blood in them, they are still cool. Their original families aren't, no; but they are fine. Pass!

You see, immigrants can be cool. It's fun to joke around with the Italians and Spanish, saying the phrases you've learned during your many summer holidays, while drinking wine from some magical valley sprinkled with sunshine and glitter. It's great to talk about New York and Seattle, and Obama and Trump, with someone who really knows their presidents, to talk about English things with your English mates, or to learn how to roll the r's in *'bonjour'* from a real French beauty. It's fun. You wouldn't like to do it all the time, but overall, these places are cool. And they are amazing for summer holidays.

Do you know what is not fun? What is not cool? Who have nothing to offer to this rich, royal UK because they come from poor, ugly countries? Eastern Europeans. These sad, struggling, non-English speaking, ex-Russians with weird accents. What could they possibly offer to GREAT Britain? Vodka, violence, and prostitutes? Ahh, get out of here, you peasants.

Yes, I truly believe that when Brexiteers say 'Fuck the immigrants', they really mean 'Fuck the eastern Europeans'. Sadly for Muslims and anybody who has a different skin colour without any English blood in them, they go under that heading as well. I really do.

I saw how people's faces changed after telling them which side of the world I was from. It went from mean curiosity to indifferent disgust. It went from 'Maybe I've been to your country. Interesting' to 'I will never go to your country, please leave'. It went from 'Do you like living in London? Do you miss home? Why are you here?' to 'Of course you love living in London, this is probably the first time you have a proper roof over your head and you make proper money. You probably send it to your poor relatives back in your poor country, so you're not really even helping the British economy.' No more questions asked, people already knew the answer.

For example, we had this gorgeous Romanian girl working in our team. An absolute beauty, I swear. Even in our sexless, bald-looking, minion costumes, she managed to get second looks from everybody around. That was until she opened her mouth and people heard where she was from. Then she was labelled a stingy gypsy, people started questioning her English language skills and her work ethics (which were both immaculate, by the way), asking her questions about what it felt like to live in a broken wooden house and share a single bed with all of her huge gypsy family. It was degrading having to watch her prove and explain herself each shift, let alone live through it myself.

After a few weeks, she stopped talking completely and just did her work; then she got praised for her skills and looks. If anybody asked her anything, she smiled and used body language to answer. After some time, people started to think she was deaf, and she never told them otherwise. It was better to be considered physically impaired than to be a Romanian, it seemed.

Another time, after doing the first rounds of drinks and bread on our tables, our Canadian colleague returned to the kitchen as pale as a corpse. She looked as though she had just served a table of ghosts. 'What happened?' we all asked, worried that she was going to pass out. It turns out that as soon as she opened her mouth, the people at her table had become so happy. 'Oh, it is so refreshing NOT to hear an eastern European accent for a change! Long live Canada!' And they tipped her a tenner to show their gratitude for her nationality and her accent. She couldn't believe it, although she accepted the money. All throughout the event, they kept tipping her tenners and praising Canada, and she had no idea how to answer them.

'What is wrong with eastern Europeans then?' I heard her anxiously ask the Romanian beauty and the Slovenian girl or boy (I couldn't tell from the bundle of clothes we were all buried in). 'What is wrong? What is happening? What is the difference between east and west that they're talking like that?' she kept asking, trying to figure out the games European politics plays and why.

The Romanian and Slovenian didn't even know how to answer. Neither did I. Even though I'm Estonian, so Swedish IKEA is much closer to us than to any of the other countries people in England labelled me from, I was considered to be a poor, ex-USSR immigrant. I had never encountered this bigotry before coming to London, yet I wasn't surprised in the slightest bit the moment I got my fair share of it.

If you live in Canada and haven't seen nor heard these things before, it can be a bit surprising. At the same time, the three of us didn't even blink an eye. Tell us something we hadn't heard before about our supposedly horrible countries, how miserable we are at home and how happy we are in England. Please do. Although I am sure I've heard it all before.

By that, I don't mean that my other fellows outside of the east were always safe. Of course not. They, too, got their fair share of bigotry, but for them it was easier to climb back up on the good ladder. Because no matter how racist the English are, they still like to spend their summers in the Mediterranean or Caribbean beaches, drink French wine and eat cheese, and go to German beer festivals. I remember when Naomi Campbell said that being a black supermodel she had had to work extra hard and give everything in order to be on the same level as the white supermodels. Well, Naomi: black – white, east – west; it's the same game, even if the colours are the same.

Our Canadian friend found out that day that George Orwell's *Animal Farm* is not only a book, but a true way of how the world works. And it was happening then, with her friends, right in front of her, not just with some strangers somewhere far away. And there's not much you can do to stop that, is there?

Well, she could have rejected the tenner and told her table what unintelligent bigots they were, but she also needed to pay her rent and not get fired. You see, at the end of the day, we are all just animals on this earth, having to live together, trying to survive, all stuck on the same lifeboat. Even though we might look different from each other, we still need one another to stay afloat and not to drown. But some animals are just more equal than the others... or so some of us like to think.

Repeat: some animals ARE more equal than the others.
Repeat: SOME ANIMALS ARE MORE EQUAL THAN THE OTHERS.
Repeat, repeat, repeat...
A repeated lie will eventually become the truth.

When I was working at the pub, I was constantly called Polish, Czech or Swedish. I knew I had a weird accent, but I guess due to my blonde hair and forever sickly-looking pale face, they decided I could be Nordic, hence from Sweden, too. When all of those guesses were wrong and they didn't know a small place called Estonia, the conversation ended.

As time progressed and the fatal June referendum vote approached, everybody started talking more and more about Brexit. People, although avoiding talking to me, would sometimes ask where I was from. 'Are you Swedish? Are you French? Are you Dutch?' All of a sudden, I was called 'the good country' names. For some reason, somehow, I had managed to break out of the 'horrible eastern European curse'. I knew the agenda behind those questions was still hostile, but they were being asked in a more subtle way, while my eastern colleagues, for example, were being met by disgusted faces and empty glasses shoved in their faces with no conversation.

When I dared to say where I am actually from, I was greeted in the same way as them. And it hurt. To see how some of your English colleagues were having good, quick yet fun conversations with the guests, and sometimes even having a laugh with them, made me jealous. I knew I could hold a conversation and banter, too. But to watch people's smiles turn into a disapproving, disgusted frown after you told them you came from a country ending with 'ia' (and it's not Australia), you might as well have died right there. You had to fill their champagne glasses and serve them delicious canapes, but be unheard and unseen for the rest of the time. The only time you could talk was to your colleagues in the dirty kitchen.

I love Estonia. And I am proud of being an Estonian. As a matter of fact, the older I get, the prouder I am. But in 2016, sometimes, in order to get through the night without constantly being looked at like you're a scary, disgusting Godzilla,

I developed a few different personalities. I am not proud of it. But I did. I became French. And ooh la, was the feedback different from being an Estonian.

When I was fifteen years old and spent the summer holidays at home, I found a French book for beginners on the shelf. I had nothing better to do at the time; all my friends were out hooking up with boys on the beach, while I was looking like a sun-allergic boy myself. So I started reading it. I did every goddamn exercise in that French book. I read countless stories of how Jules loves Francois but Francois loves cheese and wine instead. Jules then dies a horrible death from unrequited love. I learned all of it. My first words in French were love, wine, death, and pain. So, by the time the school started on the September 1st that year, I could talk about my sad life in fluent, dramatic French.

I might have had a sad beginning when it came to learning this language at the age of fifteen, but ten years later, that beginner's book with all its ridiculous stories saved me in England. I could pretend to be French and be considered someone exotic, someone worth living. That was the only time I have been happy that the English can't speak any languages but their own. Because if they had known the crap that was coming out of my mouth, they would have immediately called my bluff. But they didn't. I could make as many grammar mistakes as I wanted and use words that together made no proper sense, but still be greeted with happy smiles and *merci's*.

Am I proud of it? No. It made me feel like shit. I felt like I had put myself up for an auction and sold myself to the first taker for a hundred, whereas I was actually worth hundreds more. But sometimes, I really couldn't do anything else. I worked about 5-7 times a week and had to go through this political and geographical nonsense almost every shift, seeing people's dirty looks, hearing their mutterings. Sometimes, it really was just easier to say, '*Ah, ma petit connard. Non, je ne suis pas francaise mais je sais que vous ne connaissez aucun autre pays ni aucune autre langue, alors je continuerai. Votre education d'anglais est cul de merde et tu es rien d'autre qu'un cochon riche, alors je ne te veux pas parler, j'espere que vous etoufferez avec cette viande. Pauvre animal! Bon soiree, connard!*'

This actually translates into English as, 'Oh my dear bastard. No, I am not French, but I know that you don't know any other countries and no other language, so I will continue. Your English education is crap and you are just a rich pig, so I don't want to talk to you, I hope you choke on this meat. Poor animal! Have a good night, bastard!'

I would say this with the biggest smile as I was pouring them wine or serving them canapes, rolling my 'r's especially loud to make it sound even more exotic.

They never understood. Instead, they'd just ask for more red wine and thank me in French. If I couldn't banter with them in English (cause I was afraid of losing my job), and I couldn't speak to them in Estonian (because nobody knows it, and even if they did, it's a horrible ex-USSR country), at least I could tell them to fuck off in French. And they even loved it.

Was I ever scared of them finding out? Might there be a French-speaking Englishman at this lovely, Brexit-themed party? Somebody who had paid attention in school and learned a foreign language?

Of course there wasn't. All these events were full of older, English men who had spent their lives being proud of their country and its language, and were becoming even more proud now as Brexit was approaching. Why would they learn another language when everybody speaks theirs? And if people didn't, they should. So no, I was never even a slightly bit worried about anybody calling my bluff. I love you English fellas, I truly do, but if there's something I've learned in my time in England and on this earth it's that finding an Englishman who speaks another language is as rare as hearing an Estonian speak about their feelings. And that is rarer than the blue moon. I'll take my chances on it any day.

Soon enough, all of our lovely international team had plenty of racist stories to tell from the dinners that we served at, and we open-minded and curious citizens of this earth discussed Brexit in our dirty kitchens, too. Unfortunately, the conversations were very weird and one-sided, to be honest. The immigrants seemed to read every article and listen to all the news regarding the issue and loudly contemplate their future. The English in our team, however, 'didn't want to talk about it' or 'didn't care, because they had no opinion'. And that meant most of the discussions were just a bunch of questions and growing fears raised, instead of actually solving or talking about the situation.

The only English woman who was willing to talk about Brexit and the whole fuss about it was Rachael – a tiny, slightly older English blonde who I ended up working with almost every shift. She had been living in Portugal for the past eighteen years, had fallen in and then out of love with a sexy Portuguese man, and had just returned to London to live with her mom and dog. She would show me pictures of her dog and herself at Portuguese beaches and in the English countryside, then more pictures of her mom. Our usual pastime was cussing the managers that night, and sometimes we would even have a quick drink after work. We got along pretty well.

She was also very passionate about Brexit.

'If I could vote leave one hundred times, I would! I am so sick of these immigrants, and I can't wait for June 23rd to arrive so justice can be made again!'

Instantly, she became another person. Her usually pale face would turn fiery red and her jaw would tense up. Sometimes she would even start shivering as all this anger and hate for immigrants ran through her body. All I could think about during those moments, as I was looking at her frail, shivering body, was that I bet her face had never been that dark red even if she had spent all eighteen years in a row under the direct Portuguese sun. It was like a beetroot. It seemed like Brexit really was making miracles – more than the Mediterranean sun could ever do, apparently.

'But I am an immigrant. Are you telling me you hate me? Do you want me to fuck off? Why are you even talking to me if you think this little, so bad of me?' I asked her many, many times.

Her answer was always the same. 'No, you'll be fine, you're good. You are my friend. It's the other immigrants that get on my nerves.'

'But all immigrants are somebody's friends, that is not enough of a reason for Brexit. What makes me so special that I am going to be fine?' I'd ask.

'You'll be fine, you're my friend, you'll be fine, you're my friend,' she kept repeating.

Every time I wanted to ask her more, she'd pretend to be busy or run to the loo, so I never really found out an answer about my speciality. Still, she assured me each time that I and her other friends were going to be fine, thanks to her.

I never found out why she was so angry and what her other reasons for voting leave were. But I got to know a lot about her dog's eating, sleeping, and toilet habits, even though I never asked for that information. I could tell that perhaps she felt lonely after coming back from Portugal and didn't have many friends in England any more. I could relate to that – my own life in Estonia was in the past, and everybody I used to know was living different lives now. All my friends and acquaintances were here in England. Perhaps she was upset about her Portuguese man? Maybe he had left her and she was taking out her love pain on the whole of Europe? Oh, who knows.

But it was especially heart-warming to know that I was going to be fine in this political Brexit mess just because she was my friend. Oh, praise the Lord! Thank you, Rachael!

I know that there is a lot of things wrong with the EU and immigration is not the only reason why people started talking about getting out of it. 2016 was challenging for Europe in many ways, and one of the most controversial topics that year was the Syrian refugees. This was the spring of the dead children on the beach, frozen and drowned people running away from their homes, destroyed by war. It was horrible for everybody to see.

But it was a perfect advertisement for all the right-wing politicians around Europe to take charge and get into power. 'Do you want these refugees in your country? They can't speak the language; they won't be able to work; they will come into your country for benefits! That's what they want – to live on the benefits that *you*'ve worked so hard for!'

There were placards with queues of Syrian refugees sold as enemies all around Europe. There were talks, borders were shut around Hungary and Slovenia, preventing them from entering those countries because they were not wanted. Even Estonians were reluctant about taking refugees, saying that this was exactly what had happened 50 years before with the Russian invasion almost costing our little country its existence. People were scared – the Europeans because they felt like their countries were going to change; and the refugees because they had no idea what was ahead in their lives.

The European Union started to crumble even more. It turned out that the strong, friendly union of Europe wasn't that strong and friendly, after all. All its cracks started to get bigger and more obvious. It was the perfect time for Farage and Johnson to make their plan come alive: get out of the EU when it is at its weakest. And the union was, indeed, not steady.

Boris Johnson was driving around in his red bus with NHS slogans on it, which we all know now, just few years later, were lies. But at that time, for your usual John and Jane to read that £350million pounds went to the EU per week, was ludicrous. 'Of course, let's get out of the EU! Screw all its immigrants and refugees; we are giving away our money to them that we could support our NHS with instead! Yes, let's get out!' And they voted leave without doing any homework themselves to find out how much money actually went to whom and where.

All of my work life had become a Brexiteers' banquet, where at every shift I heard different stories about the upcoming situation. On my way to work, I always read the *Metro* and the *Evening Standard* (not much quality news there, but what's a broke girl to do?) to keep myself up-to-date with the latest news to talk about later in the kitchen. Other than the guests at my work, I never got treated badly. Nobody ever said anything racial to me on the streets or questioned my English skills – at least, not to my face.

After a while, I even got used to the disapproving faces from the guests at work, and they didn't hurt me as much any more. The more I heard their stories, the more I understood that they only saw one side of this big thing. So, I eventually stopped listening to their empty words, which were fuelled by power and hate instead of comprehension and unison, and managed to block out their cruel faces, too. I was not worried about my ability to stay in England at all. I had been here long enough to have all the details required, I had paid tax for years, and in a few months I was going to be university student in this amazing city. I really didn't worry at all.

My usual pub nights with friends became more and more political. People were talking about Brexit and the current state of the EU more and more. They were the only English people I could discuss the situation with, without them changing the subject or turning blind with rage. Still, I have to admit that the discussions were never too long or too serious, and I never really learned very much. Everybody I knew who was pro-EU never gave the referendum too much thought. In their heads, they were certain that anybody with half a brain would see through Farage's bollocks and understand his lies. Nobody knew anybody who would actually vote leave. Everybody thought it was a joke.

Well, everybody but me and the other immigrants.

I had seen and heard enough at my work to know that there was no way in hell the UK would vote to remain in the EU. I spoke to Mari, who was working in Covent Garden markets at that time. She was ready to bet her life on the UK leaving. Agatha knew as well. We would sometimes speak about it in the pub and tell our pro-EU friends that actually, this country was not very pro-EU at all. 'Ah, no way. People will know better in the end. They will know,' was their reply.

Oh well, what could we do? It wasn't like we could vote or have any say in the matter whatsoever, even though part of the reason why it happened was because of people like us – the immigrants. Eastern Europeans, ex-USSR country immigrants.

I once spoke to Agata about being Polish in the UK over a beer (or five).

'What's wrong with being Polish? I never knew they were that hated here. Why is that so?'

'Didn't you notice that before? Is that a surprise to you?' she asked me back.

'Well…' I don't know what I was about to tell her. Yes, it was a surprise. And yes, I still didn't know or understand the reason why.

Unfortunately, as our friends returned to the table, Agata quickly changed the subject and bought a new round. And that was it. We never spoke about her being Polish again. She never mentioned it either. Truth be told, I've only heard her speak Polish once, and that was away from other people.

I guess the biggest surprise was that I had even dared to ask something that was supposed to be so apparently obvious.

18

As our lease on the Upper Norwood flat was coming to an end, I decided to go back to Estonia for a few weeks. It was obvious that Paul and I had to live separately; our relationship was too broken. It was a weird time in my life, where I was stuck between the new me and the old me.

I wasn't in England on the 23rd of June. Why? Because I knew very well what was going to happen: the UK was going to vote out. There was no doubt in my or the other immigrants' minds that the result could be anything else. So, when I was buying myself a ticket back to the UK, I wondered if I wanted to be part of the shitstorm that was going to come after the 23rd of June. Were people going to yell at me without any social morals once they had, so to speak, been given a green light from the Parliament to do so?

I decided I didn't want to be anybody's punching bag based on my nationality, and chose to return to London a week later, when Beyoncé was in town, and I could work at her gig.

On the eve of the 23rd of June, when it was raining cats and dogs in London, the sky was grey and dark, and everybody was patiently waiting for the morning news, I was in Estonia, enjoying the longest day of the year with its never-ending sunset. It's the day when it stays light for 22 hours, everybody goes to the countryside, watches the fire burn, and people dance happily around it, playing our traditional old songs.

At midnight, when the moon came out for an hour, I walked home and thought to myself how I had started my first job in London on that exact date five years before. A sad, short-lived cleaning job. Five years. A lot had changed during that time. A lot was going to change again.

The 24th of June in Estonia is known as the hangover day (much like 1st of January in the UK). And even though I had been completely sober, I woke up feeling just as sick, empty, and regretful about the previous day's events. I knew the moment I went online or turned on the TV I would have to face the news from my second home, and take the beating. I'd hear all the interviews where people cheered and proudly told you to fuck off, because there was nothing holding them back any more, and I'd see Farage's smirking face as he high-fived his fellow comrades about the victory.

I really didn't want to start my day off like that; I already felt sick enough. But by early afternoon, I was forced to join social media. I kept getting Facebook notifications from my friends tagging me on pro-EU posts, and texting me how Sadiq Khan had released a statement on his Facebook wall saying that all the EU citizens living in the UK would be fine. My mailbox had three emails from the UAL promising to keep all the EU students updated as soon as more news was released.

My Facebook wall had turned into politics central, where everybody had turned into a politician, knowing what was best for their country, stating their opinions, cursing the ones that didn't vote, sharing news and pictures from others.

People were going crazy around the Westminster Parliament, whether it was as a protest or a joyous celebration. The vote result was 48.2% (remain) to 51.8% (leave). A decision that was going to change everybody's lives had been decided by basically half and half.

By 11am in the UK, many Polish shops had already been looted, and anybody who had dared to speak English with an accent had been beaten up, yelled at or mocked. Politicians from both sides were already making promises for the future: 'People in the UK made the right decision. From now on, everything will be better.' Or, 'We won't leave it like that.'

David Cameron was resigning in front of Number 10 Downing Street, looking as shocked as half the nation was, even though he was the one who had brought it up in the first place. Farage was clinking champagne glasses with his work-mates, declaring June 23rd to be the UK's Independence Day.

So, what was going to happen to EU citizens living in the UK?

'You're fucked, go home!' declared one website.

'You will all be fine, we'll fight for you,' said another.

'If you have a NANO and you have been here for five years, you'll be treated as an English citizen and you're going to be fine.'

'Finally, we can cleanse our system of the unwanted immigrants like we've always wanted to. Read between the lines: fuck off, will ya?'

I stared in horror at the TV screen, listening to all these people, my phone in my hand showing different notifications every minute, and I just cried. I couldn't help it. The tears just kept coming and coming. I wasn't crying because I was surprised at the outcome, nor was I sobbing because I was scared about my future. I cried because it felt like the relationship between me and this country, that had lasted for five long years, was fake. Throughout these five years, despite having really hard moments at times, we'd had a loving, strong relationship. The more I gave to her, the more she gave back to me. I did my duty of paying taxes and I loved its people. And for all those years, it had seemed like she loved me back, too.

This day felt like being punched in the face by your loved one. I cried because this person with whom you've shared so many beautiful, lovely moments, said the sweetest words and promises to each other, now – when given the chance – kicks you to the kerb, humiliates and hurts you in the dirtiest, easiest, most vile way ever, in front of everybody. No preparation, no nothing. Right in your damn face. The 51.8% of this person will drag you through the gutter and throw more punches at you when you're already on the ground. Over and over again. But you stay, because the 48.2% is still beautiful and loving, and you still cherish your memories together. Half is good, the other half is bad.

That's why I cried. I felt like shit for still loving the country that apparently didn't love me back and had instead hit me with a cheap shot as soon as it could. It was one thing hearing it at dinner tables; it was another to see it on the news as an irreversible fact.

Scotland, London, and Northern Ireland had the highest remain votes. Nicola Sturgeon, Scotland's First Minister, was talking about Scotland's independence referendum; London didn't want to be considered part of England any more. More and more shops were being looted, immigrants hurt. One piece of shocking news after another.

I went for a walk. I felt like I was watching *Titanic* – a powerful, unsinkable ship that had hit an iceberg called Brexit, and now everybody was trying to stay afloat in the best way possible. Some were drinking and dancing, determined that life would only get better from now on; others were already getting on the lifeboats and trying to save what they still could. Who was I? Jack or Rose? I had won my ticket five years ago in the gamble of EU migration rules and had made friends with the 1st Class passengers (English) during my stay. Now was I going to sink like Jack into the cold, racist waters? Or was I going to survive like Rose – shocked, confused, but alive?

I walked around the countryside for a good few hours, the only sounds being the neighbours' cows and the sniffs of my stuffed-up, dripping nose. I went through a whole emotional rollercoaster, as one would when they're breaking up with their lover of many years. It was a whole Beyoncé's *Lemonade* right there for me. Was I not gonna be able to go to university and educate myself, just because of my nationality? Again? Just like with the apprenticeship years before? What kind of a trick was life playing on me? More anger. More tears.

After a few hours of hanging out with the cows, I got angry at myself. What the hell was I crying for? I was never Jack; I was always Rose. I come from Estonia – a country that has given me so much and will continue to have free borders. So what the hell was I complaining about? I was in the best lifeboat of them all. It was the English that had screwed themselves over, not me.

And just like Rose, I was going to survive that Brexit iceberg. I was going to dance with the people on all decks – the highest and the lowest. So I jumped out of my lifeboat Estonia, and went back on the UK ship. There were still things I needed to take care of. My Jack, my lovely amazing friends, were all on that ship.

A week later, I was back in London. For the first time in my life, I was stopped and asked at the border where I was from and if I was in the country for business or pleasure.

'Where are you coming from? Do you work here? Are you here for a holiday?' This huge, scary guy was studying my ID card and then looking me up and down, frowning at my appearance.

Ready to be fully searched and taken to the other room, I put on my best smile and said, 'Bit of both.'

Immediately, he warmed up to me, and his stance eased up.

To my surprise, he even smiled back at me. 'Welcome. Have fun and stay safe.' And from his accent, I heard he wasn't English either. High-five, my brother-from-another-mother!

It was one week after the referendum. During this week, I had learned a new English word – bigotry. I never knew it before. I wasn't taught that at school, nor was it in any of the American TV shows I had watched growing up. Now, these two words – bigots and bigotry – were everywhere.

I spent the first week back in the UK at Mari's in east London. When she heard I was coming back, she insisted I stayed with her so she could speak and make stupid jokes in her mother tongue again, while eating tons of potatoes in one go without any judgment. It had been nine years since she had left Estonia and many months since she had spoken any Estonian.

East London is, compared to south London, fancy, clean, and quiet. For all these reasons, it's also as boring as hell. I couldn't wait to get back to the south and hang out with all the crackheads and their pitbulls in Brixton and my sweet beer and banter-loving friends. A place that was considered the most criminal and ugly in the whole city was a true gem for me. Even from my first day in London, I had heard about Brixton's bad reputation. Every time I told people where I lived, they were shocked and then said, 'Well, somebody has to live there…'

But guess what? Out of all the Brexit voters, London had the highest number of Remainers; and in London, Lambeth borough had the highest number of Remainers. So it was heart-warmingly beautiful for my sad immigrant ass to know that out of all the places in the UK, I had chosen to build my life in the most tolerant and sweetest part. Thank you, Lambeth, from the bottom of my heart.

A week later, I was living in Streatham Common. My new home was a semi-detached, two-storey house, aka the copy+paste buildings that all look the same. The only indicator of my home on this long street was the hole in the pavement in front of it, and the horribly squeaky gate that kept nobody away. Without these two features, I wouldn't have recognised my own home from the other hundred there.

It was also the first house that was completely infested with mice as well. From that moment on, I could participate in the English people's favourite joke of 'Do you have any pets?' 'Yeah, mate, got plenty of mice and rats running around me home.' Ha-ha-ha-ha. English humour. It's as funny as it is sad.

English mice are very feisty. Even the rodent repellers from Argos and all the home cats I've seen, can't keep them away.

I wasn't exactly excited about living with mice, but I had to sort out my life as quickly as possible and I didn't want to stay on Mari's couch forever. So I took whatever I could get within my budget.

I continued working for the agency; the month I had been away hadn't made any difference to my work life in London. I told ya, unless you fuck up tremendously or dare to disagree with the managers/guests, nobody really cares about you in this job. You could go off for months and they still wouldn't know you'd been away. This time, it worked for my benefit and I didn't mind being invisible at all. I had my friends at the pub who made me feel very visible and loved, despite all the crap I got outside of it.

I wouldn't say that the fancy dinners and events changed much after Brexit. People didn't become more racist or rude than they had been before. They were the same, only louder.

And the discussions would sometimes get pretty heated even between the ones who had voted the same way.

It seemed more and more as if people didn't have a real grasp of what they had actually gotten themselves into, which resulted in both sides – Remainers and Leavers – being upset with the Parliament and angry about the situation going on. People had had different understanding of what would happen after the voting. One by one, slowly but steadily, they started to get more and more angry.

'Why isn't the deal made quicker? What are we waiting for? I want it now and I want it all!' There were articles on the news about people saying they'd rather go hungry and live in poverty than spend another day in the EU. Only a privileged person who has never been hungry nor lived in poverty would say something so silly and idiotic. Morals are strong and respectful to have, but a hungry belly can make you do things that you would never otherwise even think about, especially when your children are involved. Never underestimate the survival instinct and the decisions of a hungry belly.

The closer I got to my haters, the more I started to realise that they didn't even understand exactly WHAT they were hating, who, or why. Or if they did know it in their minds, their explanations and verbal outbursts came out as totally confused. I never felt bad for what they said, although I – the eastern European immigrant – should apparently have gone and killed myself or run back to the east ages ago. Oh well, I guess I hadn't understood that part. Me no spiik Engliis, rimimber?

I had been working for the agency for the past eighteen months and knew it would be probably the best job to have when I started university in a few months. But I was happy when a good friend offered me a part-time job at the bakery she was managing. It was a local south London family bakery, with homemade sweets and fresh bread. It was a shitty pay, but it was only one train stop away from my house, and you could eat anything you laid your eyes on. That alone was good enough for me. So, I gladly accepted the job, although my blood pressure and already sensitive teeth shivered at the thought of it.

I started working at the bakery Mondays and Tuesdays and spent the rest of the week doing events with the agency. It was amazing. I ate so many cheese and onion and Cornish pasties that I gained a pound within a month of working there. I fell in love with salt and vinegar crisps (even though they still make me sneeze, it's my favourite flavour) and drank shitloads of ginger beer (that is not beer at all). I had never seen these things in Estonia before, but now they made up my breakfast, lunch, and dinner.

By the end of August, I had quit the agency. As I mentioned before, nobody even noticed I'd gone. I burned my penguin clothes and the stinky black shoes that I had been forced to wear, and let my hair hang loose. Then I started working at the bakery five times a week, baking croissants and pies (and eating half of them on the way) while listening to music, hanging out with my new colleagues, and getting ready for university. Life was good.

Our bakery was small, with a little cafe in the corner. The bakery opened its doors at 7am every morning, with the girls baking croissants and *pain au chocolat*, putting out fresh sourdough bread and the delicious cakes, doughnuts, and pastries. Coffee machine on. Sandwich boards ready. By the time I arrived two hours later, the girls had already wakened up half of west Dulwich with their coffee and bacon butties.

It was always the same. The first people to come in were the construction workers with strong Cockney accents working nearby, grabbing their morning sandwich and tea ('With at least three sugars each, love, innit, ta'); elderly people with sweet posh accents getting their fresh bread ('Oh thank you, my dear!') and local schoolkids eating doughnuts while their exhausted mothers were asking for a triple shot latte ('Ah bloody hell, I'm already late for work, please could you make that as strong as possible? Cheers, darling.').

I loved it. After some time, I got to know all the bantering construction workers and the always exhausted, always rushing mothers with their crazy, sugar-fuelled kids. I got to know who liked what type of bread and how people preferred their hot drinks and sandwiches made in a certain way. I truly loved chatting with them, talking about the whole world while I was getting their orders. It was just like it had been at the Railway years before – the regulars and your colleagues became your friends and work didn't even feel like work any more.

Speaking of colleagues, there was a pretty international team there. There were only nine employees. We had a girl from South Africa, another from Eritrea, a Spanish beauty, my sister-from-another-mister was from Lithuania, and me, of course, from Estonia. We had four English girls working with us, too. But apart from my friend who was managing the place, they were too busy with their extra curriculum things, so most of the duties stayed on the six of us, the foreigners.

We were all girls, all young, fun-loving and hard working. We had sugary pastries to keep our life sweet, coffee to keep us going, and music to shake our bums to while serving the customers. It was fun. It was exactly like what the Railway life had been, only this time we drank lattes instead of Jäegerbombs and had to watch our language a wee bit more. Instead of talking about 'your usual lager, mate, and a kiss on the cheek, innit', I spoke about gardening, raising kids, going to school, and ham and cheese sandwiches.

With a fairly small, closed ring of regular customers, we could always tell when somebody was not local and new to the shop. And you could always tell who had voted for what.

First, they would ask you if you made coffee, despite you standing next to a blinking machine and being surrounded by names and pictures of coffee. Then they would ask if there was any bread – although the whole window is full of it. Once you had answered their two questions, they would ask, 'Where are you from?'

'Estonia!'

As soon as I quit the agency, I had started hearing nicer things being said about the foreigners. Turned out, we weren't that bad after all. It turned out that the 48% were louder than I had first thought. But the round of questions wasn't over yet. As a matter of fact, the real *creme de la creme* was about to come.

'What are you doing here? I mean, why are you here? Do you study, or just work or...?' Ahhaaa! Level two. It was a simple question that held so much emotion. The way it was asked, in a curious, investigative, careful voice. The judgmental, fake friendly face they said it with. It's like when a policeman asks you what you did on a Friday evening between the hours of 7-9pm. It is a simple question without a correct answer. There's always a part one, two, and three, and by the end, you don't even know what you did an hour ago.

But as a caffeinated bunny, I was always up for a chat, always trying to be positive, and I didn't mind talking to them. Especially since, for the first time in this country, I did have a reason to be there. Enthusiastically, I would tell them that I was starting university in a month and that I would be studying journalism. 'Yes, my English is fine. Yes, I know I have a funny accent. No, my family is not here with me. Yes, I might go back one day. Perhaps when the school is over? I don't know. Yes, I am happy here. Yes, Estonia is also in the European Union. Yes, yes, yes…'

Once the interrogation was finished, they'd leave, looking pensive and worried. They rarely got the bread and coffee they asked for in the beginning, but I guess the other answers had filled them up enough, whatever they might have gotten from it.

I always knew the agenda behind those questions. Any fool could have seen it. After Brexit, it was quite normal to be asked what you were doing in this country after you told people where you were from. But I like to give people the benefit of the doubt. Maybe this guy genuinely cares about where I come from? Maybe he is actually interested in something other than putting me down? Maybe; perhaps; no; not really, though.

Although I could handle these conversations and not care too much, my co-worker Laura from Lithuania hated being put under the spotlight, and declined to answer them. If she got asked where she was from, she would ask them the same. If she got asked what she was doing in this country, she'd say, 'More than you, darling.' Laura was a tall, sweet Lithuanian woman who was very helpful and funny, yet didn't mind punching you in the corner if you rubbed her up the wrong way. She had been living in London for over ten years, had English citizenship, a car, a home, a family. The only Lithuanian thing about her was her second passport, the fact that she liked potatoes, and an accent she couldn't change. So if anybody asked her questions like where she was from and what was she doing in this country, I swear to God, all I could hope was that the other person was either strong enough not to start crying or smart enough to leave the cafe as quickly as possible. You don't mess with Laura. Simply put, you just don't. Especially when it came to the life she had built for her and her family in England over the past ten years.

Our Spanish mamasita, Magda, was asked the first question many times, but people rarely got to the second part to ask what she was doing there. I guess her beauty was too distracting. Nobody could argue with her, with her long, dark curls and her 50s' clothing style. And the fact that she was from Spain was good enough. I've already mentioned, Spain is where the English go for retirement, Spain is where the English go to see the sun, Spain is where the English go to shoot *Love Island*. To a lot of English people, Spain and Ireland are the only two places they will ever visit in their lives. Who cared what she was doing here? She's gorgeous! *Viva Espana*!

But for Laura and I, the poor ex-'Russians', it was a little bit tougher. Fortunately for me, I had the university card as my excuse and Laura had her feisty personality to get rid of anybody who dared to question our existence in this country.

September arrived fast, and school was about to start. I had my pencils, notebooks, and textbooks all ready. I was craving for education and was determined to be a better person. I was ready and counting down the days until school would start. Even the people at work were excited and rooting for me.

Unfortunately, what didn't want to come was my student loan – and without it, I wasn't gonna be able to study anything. From the moment I'd been accepted to uni in early spring, I had been dealing with the loan – calling them, sending documents, exchanging emails. But as soon as it looked like it was within my reach, it got taken away again by them asking for papers that I'd never had in the first place.

You see, due to the fact that I had been living in the UK for over five years already, I wasn't considered to be an EU candidate any more, but a home student. Five years is the magical number in this country, I discovered. It takes that many years for you to live here and then you can apply for a citizenship; it takes that many years to be called a home student, not a foreigner any more. Five years. It would have been much easier for me to get the loan if I hadn't lived in this country at all.

My battle with the student loan office had lasted for the whole of spring, summer and early autumn. But I was determined to make it work. And whatever they asked, I provided.

In Estonia, school starts on the 1st of September. It doesn't matter whether it's university, middle school, or First Grade: 1st of September is education day. In England, school starts whenever, or at least, it seems that way to me. Some kids go back to school at the end of August, others a month later. Depends on the school, depends on... God knows what.

My studies started at the end of September. The rule in university is that if you struggle with getting the loan, you can attend classes for one month, and after that, you either have to pay for the semester yourself or withdraw from uni. So I had time until the end of October to get my paperwork sorted out.

During that month, the student loan number was on my speed dial and I am sure the student advisors grew sick of seeing my face asking for their help. I attended every single class and wrote down every single detail and every word that was shown or mentioned. I met up with as many people as I could and asked them so many journalistic questions that I started to annoy myself. But I was determined to make the little time I had left work for me. I knew I was worth more than life was giving me at that moment; I was capable of doing more, knowing more. And I was not gonna let it slip away in the same way as the apprenticeship had a few years before.

After school, I'd go to work for a few hours, making sandwiches and coffee while explaining to people why I was in this country and why. Then I would go home and read the emails that notified me of the other hundred things the student loan people still needed from me and how little time I had left to provide them. I would run around sixteen hours every day, trying to sort out the issues with the student loan, taking in what the professors preached, and working at the bakery.

I felt that as long as I could stay in uni, everything was gonna be fine. University gave me a reason to be in this country so I could fight off the rascals that otherwise doubted it. I was a student. I had potential in this life. I was, theoretically, gonna be something better than I was today. I held onto that dream with all my might, and was willing to sacrifice everything I had created in London so far in order to keep it.

But my life isn't a happy fairytale. I think anyone reading so far has understood that most of the things in my life, especially when they include paperwork, documents, and becoming a better version of myself, are always difficult for me. So, of course, even though I had been in touch with the student loan people for over six months, provided them with everything they wanted from me, answered their every question, given them all my documents, showed them all of my papers… I did not get the student loan.

There was a period of twenty days back in 2013 that they wouldn't accept my UK address, so they decided I hadn't been in the UK. Twenty days. I had been living in the hostel then, working in the bar at that time; I was 100% in the UK. I even managed to come up with addresses for my squatting period, where I was actually struggling to have a home. But they chose some random time when I was completely here to be my mistake, despite me having proof of it. All the people that I spoke to agreed and understood it was an incomprehensible decision, yet said there was nothing they could do about it.

'There's different laws for the home students, and you're considered as one since you've lived here for over five years,' they all said.

It would actually have been easier for me to go to uni in England if I had never lived in England before.

I got the final letter stating 'unfortunately we have to inform you that you are not eligible...' just days before the month ended, along with the bank details where I should pay them if I wanted to continue with my studies. £9000 a year, for three years, plus the living costs. I obviously didn't have that kind of money. I could've asked my grandma – I knew she would be able to give it – but I didn't have the heart to. She was already against me being in the UK, and asking for a large sum to spend another three years in this country would have been just a cherry on an already shit cake.

Once again, I had failed. I had done everything properly, given them all the documents required, yet they still found a loophole to hold against me.

I attended the classes for the final week, still writing down everything and being as attentive as one sad soul with a dark future can be. I withdrew my papers and thanked the advisors for being so friendly and helpful. I said goodbye to the professors for all the information they had given me, and I promised them to keep on writing and keep pursuing my journalistic career.

Then I went straight to the pub and got really, really drunk. To be honest, I got completely wasted for a few days in a row. I spoke to my workmates, who felt sorry for me for not getting the student loan, but were happy because now I could work five, six, hell, sometimes even seven times a week! And when I finally got to work, still not completely sober, and anybody curiously asked me where I was from and what I was doing in this country, I told them what they all really wanted to hear:

'Me? I am from Estonia. A horrible, poor, sad, ex-USSR country. What am I doing here? I've come here just to take your job. I do absolutely nothing else in my life. I came here to take your job.'

19

~

For the student loan people, I might have been considered a home student, but for everybody else, my home was far away and I should be, too. My life was like a lose-lose situation where I was damned if I did and damned if I didn't.

Frankly, after I walked out of the university doors with the leaving papers in my hands, I couldn't give a toss any more. Instead of writing and trying to become a journalist on my own, as I had told the professors, I just kept drinking and kept none of my promises. Previously, I had always had this light blinking at the end of my tunnel, but now, the system had broken its lightbulb and I was lost in the darkness, too tired of failing all the time to gather myself together again.

I started to drink a lot on and off the job, I have to admit. Vodka mixed with Coke in a coffee cup looks exactly like black americano and doesn't smell, if you dose it right. After all, I had learned all these tricks from working in the pub where, although alcohol was your best friend, you had to make sure you were in control of the money you were handling, the customers you were serving, and your own little self at all times.

The bakery was a piece of cake compared to what I had done before. As a matter of fact, I worked better when I was drunk. I was happier, faster, less suicidal, hence more productive. And I didn't give a shit. I didn't even give a crap when people said Estonia was in Romania, that we all speak Polish and Russian, and declared that all eastern European women were prostitutes. I couldn't care less any more. I nodded and laughed along with them when they made some stereotypical Slavic jokes I was supposed to understand and educated me on what a horrible place my home was. I just kept sipping on my strong homemade coffee. I was already so low I couldn't be put down any lower.

What was the point of explaining the truth? I had explained myself, my existence, my country for years, yet every conversation always ended the same, with questions about what I was doing in this country and why I was there. No matter what I answered, they left me with a worried, judgmental look, as if I did not know my own country's history, place, or language. At the end of the day, there was only one thing they wanted to hear from me and that was to confirm all the crap that was said in the media: I do nothing, I am nothing, I have come here to take your place.

You should have seen how quickly people left the bakery now when I gave those answers to their questions. Laura' feisty personality, Magda's stunning beauty, and my intoxicated indifference to life, all saved us from the people with immigration questions.

I would say the most hurtful moment regarding the bakery and Brexit occurred one stupid morning when I started earlier than usual. It meant that I had not yet had my strong coffee, and – surprisingly – I wasn't hungover. I was serving the usual elders their bread, the mothers' coffees and their kids' doughnuts, when all of a sudden, these three huge construction guys walked in and ordered a bunch of sausage rolls.

As I was making them their teas, they were laughing and whispering to each other.

'Alright, guys, that will be £12.50, please,' I said.

'Are you Polish?' this guy asked, as half of the pastry was coming out of his mouth, tea spilling everywhere.

'Nope. 12.50 please, guys," I said again. I was too sober for this kind of conversation. Too vulnerable.

'You sound exactly like our stupid Polish co-worker! Hahaa haa!' And they all burst into laughter. All the sausage rolls they were eating were coming out of their mouths, crumbling onto the floor, tea spilling everywhere, as they laughed their arses off at their own apparent joke.

'You really are funny. You do know there are more coun-tries in eastern Europe than just Poland, right? Please, this will be £12.50. Paying cash or card?' I asked again.

But my words fell on deaf ears. They were too busy laugh-ing at their joke and were, I guess, trying to imitate the Polish language. I mean, I can't be sure – maybe they were choking on their pastries instead? I will never know.

I had to repeat myself many times before they noticed they had to pay. Finally, one of the guys took out a £20 note.

'So, *DARLING*, this is twenty pounds. Did ya know it? This is *OUR* Queen Elizabeth on it. Did ya know that? Twenty pounds, yeah? This is our queen, yeah? We have monarchy in this country, did ya know that, *DARLING*? Do ya know where you is?' This guy was shaking the note in front of me, pointing at the Queen's face, laughing and asking in broken English if I had seen this money before, while all of his friends were encouraging him with their laughter. These guys must have thought they were bloody stand-up comedians at eight o'clock in the morning. Lucky me to witness such a hilarious show.

'Oh, is it? I thought it was just some random bird,' I told him and gave back his change, when he finally decided to give me the money.

I wasn't gonna tell them that I was fully aware of where I was, what I saw, and had even met their fabulous queen face-to-face. They were too amused with themselves to hear what I had to say anyway.

He grabbed his change, put it in his dirty back pocket with his ass hanging out, and they all left, still laughing and still trying to imitate their Polish co-worker's accent and mine.

The shop looked like a pigsty. All the mud from their boots, pastry crumbs from their mouths, and drops of tea, were all over the floor, making it look as though we had just gone through an afternoon rush hour. Thankfully, it was a quiet morning and nobody else had been in the shop at that time; they would probably have been terrified and shocked about the whole thing.

So I cleaned up the place, took a deep breath, made myself an extra strong coffee with a little special elixir that I always carried around in my bag, and sat outside for a moment until the sensation of sweet alcohol and strong caffeine rushed through me.

I am who I am, and it ain't my fault they know so little about the world, I thought to myself. Maybe one day they would know more about Europe and different countries, and understand how demeaning they had just been. Or maybe one day when they go outside their comfort zone they will understand that being different does not mean being bad.

After some time, I could breathe again without wanting to cry. I forced myself to have a good day and returned to the kitchen to make some sandwiches and to talk to our nice regulars about gardening, kids, school, and the weather. Who knows? Maybe they also mocked my accent and nationality once they left the shop; maybe not. But those three guys and their little stand-up show had struck something deep inside me and I wish I hadn't had to be part of it.

On the other hand, though, if Laura had been behind the till that morning, those guys would have probably been hit on the head with ciabattas and burned with hot coffee, along with some spicy words about politics, geography, and human decency. Laura was feisty like that.

It was so lucky for those guys that it was only me. And lucky for me that alcohol exists.

Frankly, the next half a year is all a bit of a blur. I drank, smoked, and snorted everything I could get my hands on, at anytime of the day. Why not? My four-year-old relationship was over, my career was going nowhere, my every attempt at bettering myself had failed, and the country I was in blatantly hated me. It was easier to take in those punches with a bottle. It made me feel warm in my belly and numb in my head, despite the cold and ugly words that were said to my face and on the media.

I thought about going back to Estonia. I did. But I was too embarrassed and disgusted just seeing myself in the mirror, and didn't want my family to see me miserable like that. Throughout this whole time, for the past five years, they had thought I was an idiot for living far away, and I didn't want to show them they were right.

I felt like an idiot; a worthless piece of shit. Every single, damn morning. Until the second 'black americano' would slowly kick in and give me false confidence and temporary contentment. False and temporary, indeed, but I didn't care. At that time, I was so disgusted with myself that I didn't want any of my 'previous life people' to know me. I thought the only way I would be going back to Estonia would be in a body bag – and to be honest, that time didn't feel too far off any more.

At that time, London was considered to be one of the coke capitals of Europe, competing with Antwerp in Belgium for first place. Ten years earlier I had been in Estonia, where we had been competing with the Czech Republic to be the most alcoholic country in Europe. Unfortunately, we lost out to the Czechs. But in each case, I did my fair share to ensure that England and Estonia would win both 'competitions'. Well, I didn't drink much when I was 16, but I was doing everything when I was 26. I am very competitive and patriotic; what can I say?

At that time, I was living in Streatham Common, sharing a house with a Brazilian couple and some Romanian girl and boy who were never home. The house was so quiet that I spent as little time in it as possible to stop myself from going crazy. Whenever there was silence, it took only seconds for my good old demon to come out and start mocking me. This dark, unwanted friend of mine had been there from the very first day I had touched down in London, and showed its teeth to me whenever things became uncertain or unstable. After leaving the university, it had been with me every moment of the day, laughingly watching me bake the pastries, mocking me when I was having a drink, undermining me when I dared to dream for even a moment.

You're living a great life, aren't you? This is what you have always wanted, isn't it? Why are you so sad now? Did you not learn anything from your great-grandma? You will never fit in here with these people! Never! Look at your pathetic little self. Living the dream, aren't you? With every sip, that voice got louder, more demeaning, and more aggressive. But without the sips, I found it too heavy to breathe and exist. So I kept drinking until I passed out and the words and the voice didn't matter any more.

The only time I didn't run out was when the Brazilians were at home, cooking feijoada (black bean stew) in the kitchen, listening to music, opening a few beers and speaking loudly. I didn't even care what was coming out of their mouths as long as somebody WAS talking, music WAS playing, and there WAS alcohol around. But when they weren't there, I ran out. I ran to any bar that was nearby and called up any person that was around to have a drink on a Monday evening.

The Brazilian couple I lived with were very nice. They were slightly older than me and definitely much happier. Their biggest passion was travelling, and living in London enabled them to see the world cheaper, quicker, and in a more convenient way than they could have if they'd stayed in Brazil. She worked as a nanny, while he was a delivery man. Every chance they got, they would travel the world, talking to different people. Naturally, they would tell me about their travel adventures and experiences when we were spending evenings in the kitchen drinking and hanging out. I must admit, they were mostly eating, I was mostly drinking. They were mostly talking, I was mostly listening.

This house was the first place I had lived with non-English people. I had been living in England, in an English bubble for the past five-and-a-half years and, despite being an immigrant myself, I had never felt like one nor been treated as one, except at work. But as I started to listen to what the Brazilians were saying, I began to see the immigrant's side of the story as well. And their England was completely different from the one I had encountered.

They had both lived in the UK for over ten years and had met each other there. Their friends, their life, was here. They enjoyed the freedom of travelling in Europe, and the fair and uncorrupt system of the EU, so they liked living in England very much. But they didn't like the English people.

'They are cold, rude, and uptight,' they said. Working as a nanny, the woman had met all sorts of people in her life and dealt closely with them and their demands. She said it was impossible to strike up a conversation with most of them, because 'everyone likes to keep to themselves'.

I especially remember one time when she said that the English don't like their dogs touched and patted. She loved all animals and wanted a pet, but due to the renting agreements could only show her love for animals to random dogs in the parks and stray foxes in the streets. After spending ten years trying to pat strangers' pets, she had come to the conclusion that you should stay away from English dog owners, because they were rude and liked to be alone.

'In Brazil, you can strike up a conversation with anybody, anywhere, at all times. The English don't do that. The English don't know how to talk,' they both agreed sadly.

I was stunned. Even in my alcohol-fuelled mind, their comments struck home and I realised how different this country was for them than it was for me. In my experience, the English used their dogs as chick- and dick-magnets, and loved to talk about them at all times. In my experience, the English would strike up random conversations with anybody, even too much, because they hated awkward silences and wanted to chit-chat about anything with anybody just to prevent it.

Then again... I come from Estonia. We hardly even talk to the ones we love, let alone to a stranger. These Brazilians would probably suffer a lonely heart attack if they ever travelled to my country (which they won't).

For me, the English were right in the middle: not too much, nor too little. No other nation could share my dark, sarcastic humour and make me laugh harder than the English. No other nation could understand my love for beer and vodka and getting pissed in the afternoon but the English. So I loved them. I enjoyed the fact that I could strike up a conversation with anybody on the street or a pub, and joke around, even though their initial political correctness and politeness would sometimes put me off. But it was usually easily sorted by making a stupid joke, then the English would ease up immediately, turn into a bantering beast, and shove their dogs in your face to pat them.

I enjoyed spending time in the kitchen with the Brazilians, although all of our discussions about the English turned out to be the same. They stuck to their theory that even though they loved the country, they didn't like the cold, rude people living in it. I was the opposite; I couldn't give a toss about the weather or the good travelling links. I had stayed in England solely because of the wonderful English people I had met while here.

I found myself constantly trying to prove to them how nice and friendly these people could be. 'There's bad apples everywhere, but don't let those few define a whole country for ya,' I always told them. They listened, but didn't believe me. And I refused to believe them.

Still, there were times when I felt like I was defending my enemy. After all, I would spend my evenings sitting in the kitchen explaining to the Brazilians about how lovely the English were, then spent my days explaining to the English about my own existence, trying to prove to them that I was not a cold, uptight freeloader, or whatever else they considered me to be. So what was I really fighting for? Maybe, actually, the Brazilians were right. Maybe all the English were, indeed, just cold, selfish, uptight bigots who no longer had to hide their racist side after the Brexit referendum.

Were the Brazilians right and I was wrong?

Oh well. Open another beer and think less, my dear. The less you think, the happier you are.

When they weren't at home and the pubs were closed, I had to face myself alone. It was so quiet I started to love the mice running around and the sound of them eating the walls and floors. It made me feel like I was still alive. I was still living, still hearing other life around me, somebody being happy.

As I was lying in bed, half-comatose from all the chemicals in me, I wondered if they would eat me soon, too. Google says mice don't like the warmth of people so they stay away, but it was a cold and wet winter and I had hardly any blood still running inside me to provide any body warmth. I would imagine them eating me, becoming as big, powerful, and violent as rats. They would chew off my face, my toes, my fingertips, and would nibble on my eyelids. They would drink my eyeballs. When I didn't show up for work, the Brazilians I lived with would find me half eaten in my own bed. They would tell my crying mom that I had felt no pain because I was already too numb and sad from living. My grandma would have to pay for her half-eaten, zombie-looking grand-daughter to be delivered back to her home country. Neither of them would even get the horrible shirt that says 'My daughter went to London and all I got was this lousy T-shirt'. They would get a half-eaten corpse instead.

These crazy thoughts ran through my head every evening as I heard the mice chewing their way into my room. I didn't care. It reminded me of the old squatting days, my arrival in London, my first love Austin, and the way he hated the mice so much he put on David Bowie to keep them away. At that time, I hadn't cared about the little animals running all over me; I was too much in love to have eyes and ears for anybody but him. At that time, I had known nothing about the politics or bigotry.

Five years later, I had seen all of it. And it had all made me too drunk, lonely, and numb, to care. In a way, I was even waiting for the mice to come and nibble me so that I could finally feel something at least.

I must have gone to Estonia for a week in January, because there is a picture of our family all sitting around grandma's birthday table. But I have no recollection of this time whatsoever. I was home (I guess)… but not really. I do recall my mom looking at me and saying that I should get myself checked at the doctor's, as I looked so bad there might be something wrong with me. 'I feel fantastic,' I lied to her.

That was it. I can't remember anything or anybody else.

I can't recall my own birthday a few weeks later, nor any of my friends' birthdays at that time either. Time had no meaning, no real value. I worked on the weekends and weekdays and partied just as hard, so it didn't really matter whether it was Monday or Saturday – work, vodka, and coke were always there, along with the everlasting cold, grey weather.

Nobody ever asked me any questions at work. Funnily enough, the only time my colleagues questioned my sobriety was on my sober, hangover days. Then they could smell the stale alcohol and see my swollen eyes, and would ask me what was going on. Otherwise, I fooled them all. I even fooled myself.

I could be drunk, high and/or puking my guts out into every bush and road sign on my way to work, having had no sleep, but I always got there. Always. I never called in sick or was late. 100% working, 100% on time. I had learned how to work on autopilot at the Railway, to find stability in my conversation, and to do maths even when I could barely keep my eyes open. So, nobody ever questioned anything.

I knew what I was doing was wrong. Congratulating yourself with a beer if you haven't had a drink for a day, is not really the right way to live. But it was so easy, because there was always something happening in London and everybody's lives were so messed-up they were always up for a drink.

I remember sitting in Wetherspoons one evening after work, reading a *Metro* newspaper I had picked up on the train. In my defence, I had gone home initially, but the Brazilians weren't there and I wasn't ready to face the silence and my problems just yet. So, as I was at the pub, sipping beer, surrounded by older English men who wished I wasn't there, I read an article about this big, old psychic from the US who had come to London to heal the sad English nation. 'Y'all drink too much. Y'all drown your problems with alcohol, creating more problems. Stop drinking and all will be solved,' he said in the headlines.

I almost laughed. Londoners drink a lot? Yeah, no shit! It doesn't take a psychic from another continent to come and tell us something we can all clearly see ourselves. The English are a drinking nation. I spent the first one-and-a-half years of my UK life running around being lonely, until I ended up in a pub, started drinking, and found friends for life. If I had known that all I had to do to find friends was go to a bar, I wouldn't have had to jump on crowded buses to get some sort of human contact in order to feel alive again.

I do wonder if that US fella ever helped anyone. I mean, he was right and everything, but it takes more than just somebody's good thoughts and prayers to get over your destructive shit. He certainly didn't make me change my habits, although it was good to read some different news from the usual Brexit circus.

Besides being an unwanted immigrant, I did have something in common with the English: our love for drinking, and the tendency for self-destructive ways.

20

The friends I made while working at the pub were friends for life. We spent a lot of tme together, talking about different things, serious and funny. They were the reason I stayed in England for so long, and they were the ones I went to when the media and some customers at work advised me to 'go back home'. These people had become my home.

Yet for some reason, when it came to my own dark times, I didn't want to include them. Maybe it was my Estonian side that likes to keep everything private and not show any vulnerable emotions to anybody. Or maybe it was that I just didn't want anybody to see what a miserable, empty shadow of my former self I had become. I was ashamed of my life and didn't know how to express in words the mess I was in. Either way, I drank with them often, but never spoke about the war going on inside me. As I think we all do, there's always a part of yourself you keep hidden away, even from those closest to you.

Months went by and spring arrived again. Instead of only drinking at pubs with my mates, we also drank 'in nature' – aka, in an overcrowded Brockwell Park. This is an Englishman's way of chilling and recharging their batteries after a week of working in the city. But as an Estonian, this park chill felt as busy and anxious as being in the middle of Regent Street during rush hour.

For me, nature means going to either the forest, beach, or lake, with hardly any people around you at all. In London, nature means something completely different; anything with two trees and a little bit of grass could be counted as a 'piece of nature'.

Parks are fun, though, because you can play games and enjoy the sunshine while having G&T in a can. I spent most of my time drinking cider under the trees, away from the sun, and calming my ever-increasing anxiety so that I could function as a normal person in this English 'nature'. Even though I was drinking less alcohol, coffee, and snorting fewer lines than I had during the winter and early spring, my anxiety and a constant feel of panic remained and I didn't know how to get rid of it. If I had to be around people, I had to have a drink or two to calm my nerves. If I was alone, I would hide under a blanket, cry, and pray for this feeling to be gone. Unfortunately, neither method worked.

Whenever I felt down in London, I assured myself that I would be fine, because I had Estonia, too. My sisters, my grandmother and mother were there. My childhood friends, my cat and dog. It comforted me that the buildings in my town hadn't changed since I was born, the foods were still labelled the same way as they had been a decade before. I could fuck up in London, but I would always have a second chance in Estonia, where I was supposed to naturally fit in. Estonia was my foundation, and it was strong, steady, untouchable. The house I had built on it – London – was at times shaky and had big cracks in it, but as long as the foundation itself was strong, nothing could break the house.

I had spent the last six years in London. Once or twice a year, I had been to Estonia, where I hung out with my family and some friends, ate homemade potatoes, went to the sauna, and then left for London again. Besides those few times a year, Estonia existed only in my head and on the Internet; nowhere else. I couldn't speak the Estonian language or life to anybody around me, because they had nothing to do with it – and nor did they seem to care. I always thought that I didn't care either, and that it didn't matter.

Even though the first day of any trip back to Estonia was awkward, unusual, and almost severely uncomfortable, it wouldn't take me longer than two days to get used to my old ways. And it was the same scenario when I returned to London. I had to be two different people in those two different countries. The things I did in one country didn't apply in the other. Depending on where I was, I had to switch those two sides to the right place. That is part of the deal when living abroad, when being an immigrant. You're always half and half, never fully whole.

I'd had six years of playing this game and I had gotten used to it pretty well. However, when I went to Estonia for a week in August, hoping to be pampered and nurtured back to life, everything had changed. And when I returned to London this time, I couldn't brush off my feelings and get used to the new life in just two days, as I had previously.

Actually, things had changed one by one during the last few years, but I guess I had been too busy running around explaining my country that I failed to notice. Finally, now, when I needed the comfort, stability, and care of the nest I had come from, I understood that I had lost that nest a long time ago. I had left my foundation on its own for too long, and it had developed cracks and mould from my carelessness.

I had changed, and life in Estonia had, too. Unfortunately for me, we had changed into two completely different things. My dog didn't recognize me even after spending a few days together. My little sisters, who had been seven and four when I first left, weren't children any more— they were thirteen and eleven, grown-up girls with strong personalities. My mom's and grandmother's lives hadn't changed, but their faces had;

they were older, more tired, and for the first time in my life I understood that they would not be here forever. My great grandmother had passed away a few years before, but I'd spent her funeral day working an extra long shift at the bar in London to keep my mind off it. My Estonian friends had new friends and lovers whom I knew nothing about; they had their own hangout and lives where I didn't fit in.

These things don't happen overnight. They had taken place in the last six years while I had been away. 'Life doesn't like an empty space – it will always fill it with something unless you do it first' is a saying we have in Estonia. It looked like my space had been filled with things a long time ago, even though I had foolishly thought I still had it. Now, as I finally opened my eyes again, I could see what a superficial acquaintance I had become to it all.

My own family had become distant. I felt like the auntie that comes by once every blue moon, brings a pack of gifts and tells stories from a faraway land, before leaving again. And you just smile for the time being and say, 'All is good, life is great!' and then move on with your not-so-great life until she happens to be back in town for another set of stories.

But I wasn't their auntie – I was their sister, their daughter, and granddaughter. They were my rock, my nest, my anchor I knew I could lean on in my chaotic life. For them, I was the ever-changing weather you shouldn't pay too much attention to or get too involved with. If something was wrong at home, I was the last one to know – if ever. Don't get me wrong, in a way that makes sense. What could I have done or how could I have helped them if I was thousands of miles away? I didn't tell them about my problems, either, because I didn't want to worry them about something they couldn't fix. But that lead to… what? Petty, superficial conversations with the ones you love the most, and seeing fake smiles each time you met up.

This rock, this idea I had held onto throughout my years of change, this happy, stable place that had kept me grounded and calm while I was adventuring in London, had changed so much that now it felt wrong to call it my own. I had nothing to do with the new side of it; I didn't fit in. It wasn't my home any more.

My foundation was just a block of cold, cracked stones, crushed together, that had nothing to do with me.

All of my friends in England had grown up in south London. They had gone to the school nearby, they knew the neighbourhood, the people, and the system. With a few exceptions, my friends had all been born in this place, grown up in this place, and looked as if they were going to stay in this place until the end of their time. They were happy like that. I mean, as happy as anyone can be. When we were at parties and felt nostalgic, they'd put on music from the 90s – TLC, Britney, N'Sync – and sing away to their childhood classics, remembering the good old times when life was simpler and sweeter, along with shots of vodka and cans of beer.

But their streets weren't my streets. I had come here in my twenties and forced my way in through thick and thin, to have what they'd had from the beginning. I loved hearing their stories as we walked around their childhood streets, feeling as if I had been part of the memories all along. Soon enough, I stopped mentioning my 'previous life', because there was simply no point in explaining things they couldn't relate to. And overall, I had come to England voluntarily, so it was my decision to learn the rules of this new life and forget the previous one.

When I felt nostalgic, I listened to something in Estonian. Any song, however bad, any show, however awful, made me feel like a ten-year-old child again, to the point when sometimes a single word in its language could make me tear up. Through those crappy videos, I could live out my Estonian self and assure myself that we *ARE* a country and we *DO* exist, despite what the rest of the world thinks, knows, and will ever understand.

But the truth was, when I returned from Estonia that August, I was shaken. I didn't know what I was any more, or where I belonged. Supposedly as an Estonian, I should have felt great in Estonia, right? Well, then why didn't I? Why did I feel even lower than before? In Estonia, people believed, 'She feels better in England now, she'll stay there', but that wasn't true either. I had two addresses in two different countries, yet felt homeless, floating somewhere in between, never fully belonging to either place.

Frankly, I had felt like this for a long time. Brexit had shown England to me in a different way, and introduced me to racism and bigotry in ways I thought had been abandoned in the mid-20th century. Unfortunately, it was the beginning of the 21st century and the same feelings were all still there. All of a sudden, I understood what my great grandmother's friends meant when they had said there is 'us' and there's 'them'.

At the same time, I noticed how Estonia had become a much more liberated, cool, and interesting place than before. Our open borders meant more diversity; more diversity meant more opportunities; more opportunities meant more successful, happier people, which resulted in a better life overall.

They say you can take a man out of the country, but you can't take the country out of the man. No matter how much you might change your surroundings or your lifestyle, there will always be a part of you from the previous life that can't be killed. No matter how much you might try, or want.

I had always wanted to live abroad, so when I did that at twenty, it felt like a logical step forward. I had nothing to lose and yet so much to gain. But as time went on, I felt less and less happy.

One of the reasons why Paul and I had stayed in our toxic relationship for so long had been due to the shared misery. I had come from Estonia and left behind the life as I knew it, creating a completely new reality for myself in a new country. And Paul had done the same when he had left Australia.

I didn't want to bother my friends with my depressing stories. It was my decision to come to this country, it was my duty to deal with all these emotions. Nobody forced me to buy the ticket, nobody is forcing me to stay in this country. If you're so damn miserable, leave! You would probably make everybody happier that way.

But there's a catch. You will never feel whole any more. Once you've passed a certain level, there's no going back to the old ways. You cannot unsee what you've seen, unfeel or unknow the things you've had to learn. Go home, go.

But where is home? It isn't where I came from; it isn't where I am.

After I returned from Estonia, I became more aware of my past in Estonia and London, and started thinking more about life in general. I didn't care about going to parties or even to the pub any more. Drinks wouldn't make me drunk, they just gave me a headache. I was yearning more, I wanted more, I craved for something different. Unfortunately, I couldn't figure out what that something was.

So I fell deeper and deeper into my dark thoughts, battling with the mocking voices in my head, fighting daily with my anxiety. My priorities had changed; I had changed. I had come to this country, entered this game, without any previous experience or knowledge about how it works. I had learned everything – the tricks, the hints, the shortcuts, and other players; I had lost multiple times and won even more. Yet I wasn't happy. My main game – the one that was my beginning and was always going to be the end – wasn't mine any more. And if you don't have that, nothing else even counts.

I guess you could say I went a bit crazy. It happens after a long time of not sleeping, not eating properly, and having multiple panic attacks a day. I couldn't think clearly any more, I couldn't focus, I couldn't be. I quit my job at the bakery and stayed away from my friends. I was too dark and messed-up, and they did not deserve to be dragged into this miserable, eerie hole with me. How could I explain my homesickness to people who have never had to leave theirs? How could I explain to them the constant feeling of incompleteness, no matter where I was or what I did? I didn't want to take them down with me, so I just stayed away.

I got a job for the Christmas period in the IMAX cinema in Waterloo, and it was the only time nobody ever asked about my nationality or made any 'hilarious' jokes about it. I didn't even know this kind of work environment could exist. Then again, what is there to talk about in a dark room when *Star Wars* is on the big screen five times a day, and the whole place smells of popcorn? Somebody's nationality is the last damn thing on your mind when you're more focused on not choking on your popped corn while watching Princess Leia run around space. And I was more focused on holding myself together, trying to find meaning to my life, something to hold onto.

But once the new year came around, my new job went, too. When I returned to Estonia for a week in January, as I always had, I was greeted with the same superficial questions, everybody pretending to be good, and everything seemingly fine. Everything except me. And after fighting it for years, I broke down in my mom's car.

I didn't want what I had, and I didn't know how to get out of it. I had always thought that before I could return to Estonia, I somehow needed to prove myself, to have done something great, no matter for who or how little the deed. I needed that proof, some sort of accomplishment before I was allowed to go back. Otherwise, what's the point of it all? Otherwise, what was the point of me? Otherwise, what would I say to my family about my return? In the beginning, I had purposely stayed there so they could be proud of me for not giving up too soon on yet another thing, but years had gone by and I still hadn't given them a reason to be proud.

'Well, don't you think you've already done enough? What is it that you think you must accomplish there? You've been away for almost seven years and you ask why your sisters don't know you, why your whole family and your childhood friends feel distant to you, why you don't feel like you fit in any more. But you've been away for seven years – not seven months. Life happens. Everybody's gotten older and changed accordingly. Your grandmother is older and her health is not the same, your sisters are older and aren't children any more, I am not able to do all these things that I did seven years ago, either. That's life, this is how it works. You've been away for so long, doing your own thing. But just because you created a new life there doesn't mean that the one here stops. I just hope that whatever it is that you do there is something that makes you happy and is worth it, no matter what it is,' my mom said while I was having a nervous breakdown in front of her.

It was -23 degrees outside on this dark winter evening, and there was not a single soul outside but us. We were sitting in her car, me balling my eyes out and her keeping the engine on so it wouldn't freeze, while telling me the truth about my family – something I should have already known, yet didn't. This was the first time in about ten years that we had actually spoken candidly about life, decisions, and their consequences, for over an hour straight. And when she said the last part about me supposedly being happy, I understood that I hadn't been happy in years.

An hour later, the engine was dead and I was dehydrated from all the water that had come out of me. My mom was pissed off. Normal nagging family life resumed. But I had changed, too.

I guess it really was time for me to go back to where I came from.

I gave myself six months before I would return to Estonia for good. That would be enough time for me to make amends and give myself a last chance to make sure it was not some crazy, hastily-made decision.

I moved into a house with two English and a Lebanese girl. This was perfect for me, as I could make my stupid English jokes and practise French at the same time. I started working at the events again, although it was a bit different this time. I was mostly working as a barista in Google, occasionally still going to the Oval Cricket ground to be a barmaid, or serving dinners at weddings.

I even met Nigel Farage at the Oval one time. I knew who he was immediately, as our eyes met, and I could see from his face that he knew that I knew, too. The big, loud politician he had always tried to make himself look like on the telly was not the guy who was standing in front of me at that moment, asking for a gin and tonic. Instead, it was this very weird, nervous boy, who didn't know how to get away from this stinky situation. After all, he was about to be served by a disgusting eastern European.

Throughout these five months I went through heaps of yes's and no's, shoulda-coulda-woulda scenarios, panic and resolution, good and bad. Now that I was back in England with my second family, it was hard to imagine myself anywhere else. Until the next phone call from Estonia, or a sight of other families, and then I'd crumble into pieces again. But once it hit another summer and I had suffered the hundredth panic attack that week, I decided not to fight it any more. It had been seven years.

It wasn't easy. I didn't even tell half of my friends that I was leaving because I simply couldn't bear to say those words or to face the reality. I was convinced that I would be back in six months, before Brexit went ahead in March. I just needed a little bit of time away from this city, but I never planned to leave it.

After all these years and the people I had got to know, I simply couldn't imagine leaving it.

ACT III

~

THE RETURN

21

I had come to London with one little backpack, but it took me three flights and countless numbers of bags to bring everything back to where I had started from: my guitar that I had used for busking in Westminster and that had fed me for a while; my clothes that I had used as pillows while squatting; all the books I had been given for Christmas or bought on my numerous visits to charity shops and Waterstones.

With all my possessions gathered over the last seven years brought back with me to Estonia, everything was gone from London. And I was back to where I had started more than seven years before.

It took me two months to unpack my ten bags once I was back in Pärnu, Estonia. Not because it would have been difficult, or I was busy – no, I had all the time in the world. I just simply couldn't do it. Facing the reality and the past, mixing them together, understanding the times and my place and changes in them, just felt too much. I had spent twenty years living in this Estonian town imagining my getaway and thinking everything would be better once I returned… if ever. But I had left, and I had returned. And nothing was better.

You'd think I would have been happier, calmer, better than before, but the truth is I just felt even more conflicted. It felt unreal, bizarrely surreal to be back where I had started from, and to have lived through everything I had – yet I had nothing to show for it. It felt as if I had closed my eyes when I was nineteen and made a wish, fallen asleep, and dreamt all of this life. Now, I had wakened and opened my eyes again – and I was back in the same place, only older.

I hadn't managed to build a sensational career; I didn't have a spouse, or any other love any more. My friends – the other half of me – were in England. And I felt incomplete, weird, numb. It had been hard to mould myself into the English life-style, but now I had to mould the new me into what I had once been – and this was even harder. Everything I had learned in the last seven years felt like completely useless information which had nothing to do with the world I was now living in.

My grandmother was happy I was back, and she showered me with food. I spoke to my friends, who promised to take me around town as soon as they had time. I spoke to my sisters, who promised to hang out as soon as they could. My mother was busy with her new job. I walked my dog, who years before had run around on the beach like a puppy, but now was so old I was even walking faster than her.

I did go out. In order to prevent myself from going completely crazy, I went out every time anybody asked me. But it only caused problems. I was too loud, too opinionated, and I talked too much. I got into arguments almost every time I set my foot out of the house. People in London were fierce, strong, and not afraid to stand up for what they believed in, especially my friends. Through them, I had learned how important it was to be courageous and fight for your rights and beliefs, go on strike, if necessary. So, I had gotten used to this freedom of self-expression.

Back in my small home town Pärnu, I almost got beaten up for expressing myself. My views on the world and my place in it (whether as a woman or a person who had lived abroad) were looked at differently, and I stood alone with these thoughts. It was a jungle out there – and I was too loud, too different, too expressive for the locals. I guess in a way, they, too, expressed themselves; it just so happened their way was exactly the opposite of mine, and I was the only one with my 'silly thoughts'.

Seeing my English friends on social media felt like some long distance shadows whose voices and homes I had known, yet were now a past life, like a mirage that had never actually happened.

It is funny, isn't it? I had left London and returned to Estonia to be with my family, my friends, the Estonian life. But once I arrived, I stayed away from everybody and watched stupid English shows all day and all night. I even started to appreciate *Love Island*, horrible as it is. An English accent, pictures or movies shot in London, all melted my heart the same way Estonia had while I had been in the UK. The Sainsbury's and Tesco's logos, the M&S Christmas ads, the semi-detached houses, the silly songs. It didn't even matter what words were said, just the accent and old familiar images brought all the memories rushing back, and my fragile body instantly felt so much it didn't know whether to break down and cry or be happy and smile.

I did go to Tallinn a few times to meet my friends. Like every capital city, it is completely different from Pärnu. There are more people, international visitors, bigger parties, and hordes of wasted English bachelors still trying to get laid. Every weekend night, you could hear them around the Old Town, spilling drinks on the cobblestoned streets and trying to catch some ladies.

'Oh my God, Eva, and you love the English? Is this what you like? Is this your perfect husband?' my friends would ask me, pointing at a guy wearing a football shirt in the middle of the winter cause he'd lost his coat, spilling beer all over the streets because he was too drunk to hold his cup properly (nor did he know that public drinking is illegal). His friend was puking behind the dumpster, and he was asking 'WHERE ARE YOU LADIES GOING?' in his lovely Cockney accent. It really was a beautiful sight to see. My friends were laughing at the poor guys and at me, because I'd told them how English guys were so cool. 'This is what you want then, Eva? How did you manage to live with people like that for *SEVEN* years?'

'They aren't actually like that,' I'd tell them. We really don't get to see the best version of the lovely Englishmen in our cobblestoned Old Town.

'Yeah, right! Seven years of this, eww,' was their answer. And we would leave the poor guys alone with their drinks and dreams.

After feeling like a cuckoo, drifting between reality and dreams, sleep and wakefulness, I felt like my whole London life had been just a fairytale I had heard somewhere through the grapevine. These seven years had been just one big, beautiful, yet bittersweet fairytale.

----December

----January

----February

----March

22

'When are you coming back to London?'

'What's up, what's up?'

'Have you already bought a ticket back yet?'

I did have a ticket back to London. After the last half a year of feeling weird and incomplete, I was waiting to return to the place I knew the best. I knew how to get a job in London and I was excited about seeing my friends again. It had been six months since I had last seen them – the longest spell of time during those years of knowing each other. I missed our jokes, our nights at the back garden of the Railway, the walks around West Norwood, our bantering. There hadn't been a day when I hadn't thought of every single one of them and wished they could have been where I was and seen what I saw.

But I was terrified of coming back to living in London. The simple thought of being in this city, pushing and fighting for my spot on the overcrowded train so I could go to a home shared with other three or more people, made me shiver. It made my heart go mad, my hands sweaty, and my anxiety go instantly through the roof.

I couldn't go back. I simply couldn't live this life again.

Even if my heart said yes and dreams of hanging out with my friends made me happy, my body refused to even think about living like that again. I had spent the last eight years of my life living with other people and running around like crazy; it was what I had wanted then. It wasn't what I wanted any more.

All of these thoughts and feelings sent me into frenzy, and the little confidence and self-love I had built up in the last few months, just vanished in seconds. There hadn't been much to start with, to tell the truth. You can't mend in months something that has been broken for years.

'Are you coming?'

'Brexit is on the 29th of March. Finally we'll get rid of those idiots.'

'When will you be here? I can't wait!'

'Where you from? Why are you here?'

'We'll go and have beers and you can tell me all about what has happened in the last months!'

'You've come here to take our people's jobs!'

'I miss you so much. I'm so happy you'll be back!'

'Piss off, immigrant!

My ticket was for the 26th of March, just a few days before Brexit should have gone through.

I tried to come up with any other good reason for staying in the UK apart from the people that I had met there. Something that I could only get in London, but not in Estonia. Something besides those beautiful Railway people that I could hold onto in my times of despair. Anything at all.

I thought about it for long time. Then I cried in the shower and read a few pages of inspiring quotes to get myself worked up and motivated for the next chapter in my life in London. Then I went and cried some more, because none of that shit was helpful.

And then I decided that my life in London was truly over. I bought a ticket to return to Estonia just one week later. In that one week in London, I was going to meet all my friends, drink beers and Jäegerbombs with them, have all the walks and chilling in the parks and the back of the pub, like we usually did. I was going to collect the last few bags I had left in London, then come back and build up my life in Estonia, like I should have done ages ago. Just like my childhood friends did years ago. Just like all the Brexiteers had always wanted me to do.

As soon as I got back to London, it felt as if no time had passed since I'd been there. And at the same time, it felt like it had been ages. It was exactly the same feeling I had experienced whenever I returned to Estonia for a week throughout those seven years.

Overall, the streets were just as busy, the weather was just as grey, my friends were just as lovely as they had always been. But the streets were also dirty and the traffic insane, the place was crowded with so many people, smells, and places, it felt chaotic. I had lived seven-and-a-half years in a city that I now was struggling to even spend a week in.

Knowing that it would be ages before I would ever return to this country again, I decided to wander the streets and gain full closure for those years we had spent together, London and me. Funnily enough, it really did feel like we had been in a relationship. It had been tough at first, but I had made it love me. Unfortunately, it had then eaten me up to the point where I had felt that I had lost myself completely – and that's when you know you should get out.

Well, now I had come back to see my ex with a new look and a new mindset, on my way to a new relationship. Farewell, my lover. Farewell, my former life.

I spent the evenings with my friends, but I spent the daytime by myself, going back to the time when I had just been a kid in a big city before I met my second family. I went back to the places I had been squatting in, just to see my old homes.

I knew the place in Crystal Palace was not a squat any more, because I had passed that place many times over the years. It was a 'normal' building with 'normal' tenants now. I had also seen the place up north where our newbies squat team had been kicked out and almost killed at the hands of the Russian axe mafiosos. I had seen it every time I took the night shuttle bus to Stansted Airport to catch the 6:45 am flight to Tallinn. This was also now a 'normal' house with 'normal' people living in it.

The squat in Elephant and Castle, where we spent our first Christmas, was still a squat. Every time I passed the place on a bus, or had a longer break from university, I had gone to that street to have a look at the house. And it always warmed my heart to see that it was still standing strong.

So I went to the places I had previously called home but hadn't been near in almost eight years. After the fiasco with the Russian mafiosos, Austin had taken me to the abandoned nightclub in Greenwich Cutty Sark. Now, it was a fancy restaurant that charged more than £5 for a pint and £15 for a burger. They had beautiful dining chairs and wooden tables right where we used to have our mattresses and sleeping bags. The place was now light, loud, and fancy. Back then, there had been nothing but the sounds of our voices, the waves on the Thames, and the light from the tens of candles we always had burning. But at least now you wouldn't have to be afraid of drinking water from the tap and you could enter through the beautiful front door, not by a hole in the back the way we did.

It was harder for me to find the previous squat in Woolwich Arsenal. I thought I had gone to the right place, but the building complex looked completely different, so I was unsure. Everything was new, clean, and looked safe. There were no eleven-year-olds selling drugs on the streets any more. The only thing that was still there was the small mini-market shop on one of the corners. It still looked as shady as it had eight years before, when I had been buying beer and quick noodles before entering my room with its cold cement floor and furniture covered in birdshit. Back then, the shop had been a safe haven in an otherwise dangerous and creepy street.

The tables had clearly turned, though. I guess the eleven-year-olds had all either grown up and become wiser, or were either in the clink or six feet underground. Who knows? Either way, the Foxtons and Newington Estate agencies had gotten their claws into Woolwich Arsenal and cleaned up the place, which I guess is not a bad thing at all when you think about the safety of the streets. I just hoped that the people living there were still able to pay rent AND put food on their table, without it immediately killing their budget.

I took a DLR back – the magic train that runs without a driver – just as I had always done during my first year when I lived in Lewisham, Greenwich, Surrey Quays, and Woolwich Arsenal. The same monotonous female voice, which explained what the next stop was and reminded you to take all your belongings with you, brought back all the old uncertainty, fear and exhausted emotions I had experienced at that time. I was happy to be out of DLR.

I also wanted to go and see Bobby (Michel). Even after eight years, he was still playing the same songs in the same spot where we had met for the first time. For years, I had avoided that exit of this station where I knew he'd be busking, although I'm not exactly sure why. Now, I went there just to see him.

And there he was, with his broken guitar, long, black Rasta hair, colourful jacket, and loud voice singing how 'every little thing is gonna be alright'. I walked past him and our eyes met. I waved.

He looked startled, and stopped playing for a minute.

'Oh!' he said.

'Hey… how's it going?' I asked, as a true English person does. The only difference was, I actually wanted to know the answer.

'Good, good. You alright?' he answered, as a true Englishman does.

'All good.'

There was a moment of silence. I wanted to ask him for a drink afterwards, to thank him for everything he had done back then, and to make sure that he had eventually found a good place to stay. I wanted to…

'Alright. Gotta play while there's people. You alright, yeah? Alright then,' he quickly said. Then he adjusted his guitar, gathered himself, and started playing again as if nothing had happened. Oh, how times had changed.

'Bye, Bobby,' I said, and left.

To me, he will always remain Bobby, no matter what his actual name is. At the end of the day, if it hadn't been for him, I don't know how my London life could have even existed. So I thank him for that.

After these trips to the past, I went back to my home, to my family in Brixton. I had drinks with them in the back garden of the Railway, I hung out with them in Brockwell Park, and went for walks around south London. And a very strange thing occurred this time in the pubs. I mean, it was Brexit week, so it was on everybody's minds.

But after a few pints, strangers would start talking to me, asking, 'Why are you the way you are?' I kid you not. They didn't ask any more what I was doing in their country; no. They asked me why I was the way I was.

It seemed that they had voted for Brexit, given me the middle finger when they had heard my accent, yet now bought me a pint and asked me this question. And what they really meant was, 'Why do you speak good English? Why do you know English things? How come you're hanging out in a pub, like all of us English do? Why?'

We would speak for a long time, buying each other rounds, with me answering their questions on immigration, eastern Europe, and my life here and there. It was very difficult for them to understand that they could actually enjoy a conversation with an immigrant, after voting to get rid of them. They couldn't comprehend why I *WASN'T* a non-English speaking, weird prostitute, nor a waitress (what else do eastern European women do, right?), but just a completely normal girl that loved to drink beer and banter all night long, just like they did.

That happened a few times. Apparently, my existence came as a surprise to many people, and the situation seemed especially relevant that week. It was funny and surprising, but showed me that racism and bigotry are only triggered by the unknown. My friends didn't even know what to answer to these ridiculous assumptions, but they enjoyed the free pints.

Bobby had always told me that racism and bigotry were the outcome of unknowingness. Without knowledge come assumptions. Assumptions that, unfortunately, most of the time don't hold water with their truth, but that some people still hold onto strongly – because they simply don't know any better. People don't like the unknown, so they always try to make things understandable for themselves by using random examples. Sometimes they can be quite right, but most of the time it is better to do a little neutral research before you start labelling people.

'If either of us would be racists or bigots, we couldn't have the experience we're having right now. Imagine how much you would miss out on life just simply because of your assumptions? Simply because you assume it is something else, hence will never give it a try?' Bobby would always tell me, as he lit up another smoke.

And the man was right. I was a tiny, little, white girl and he was big, tall, black man. If we had judged each other by our appearance, Lord knows where I would have ended up in 2011. He had offered me a home at a time when I had no money and no knowledge of what I had actually gotten myself into. If he hadn't done that, would I still have stayed in London? Could I have ever met the people I now called my good friends? Lord knows. But I wouldn't change the experience I had for anything in this world.

It's been over a year now since I left London, and I've been properly back in Estonia. I got myself a job in a big international finance company that the whole world thinks started in London because its main office is there, but was actually founded by Estonian guys.

My job is being a customer support and to pick up phone calls from all around the world whenever people have any questions regarding their funds. After I've helped them with their finance issues (and also sometimes anger management), one of the questions is also:

'Where you from? You have a very interesting accent.'

'Estonia. You are calling to Estonia right now.'

'Oh, where is that? Romania, Australia? What language do Estonians speak?'

'Right under Finland, next to Russia. And we speak Estonian.'

It has become an ongoing joke in the office about where Estonia is and what language we speak there.

'Ooh, I never knew that!'

Not many people do. As soon as I've finished the phone call explaining to people how banks work and what Europe's map looks like, I hear somebody else behind me do exactly the same. And another one behind that person. And somebody next to me, or in front of me, too.

My co-workers and I explain to people who call us all day long where we are, who we are, what we do. But actually, half of my co-workers are not even Estonian. There are people from all over the world – Nigeria, Australia, Brazil, Russia, the US, the UK, Costa Rica, Sri Lanka, Korea, Japan… you name it, we have it. And they have all come to Estonia either for this job or for love.

At a time when I left my life for London, a lot of Estonians left their homes, too. And now they've returned home with goodies from around the world. We have heaps of local businesses growing into international ones that need employees. Since there's only 1.3million of us in this country, we need the foreign workforce. And they don't mind coming, it seems. Because living in Estonia is nice. It's quiet, it's small, it's safe, and the wages aren't that bad.

It was hard for my colleagues to understand at first how little I knew about Estonia, even though I am Estonian. People would come to me to ask about the tax system and healthcare in this country, and they didn't believe me when I said I knew just as little as them. In order to understand my first pay check, I had to have my Sri Lankan team lead explain how much and what we were paying for in this country for taxes.

'Where have you been? How come you don't know your own home country?' is usually the question I get asked. But I tell them I spent the last seven years in London, and if there's anything they need to know about the UK's tax system or the NHS, or any good places to go out in London, I can help them with that.

'SEVEN years? What the hell is there to do in England for SEVEN years?!' is always the second question. Unfortunately, the answer of 'I met some amazing people and time just flew' is not a good enough response.

'I don't know about the English being amazing, but I do know they are bigots who love to get wasted in pubs and shout and demean you on the phone,' I am told. And I usually leave it at that.

Now that I'm living in Estonia, the kind of people that represent the UK here are either drunk bachelors in the Old Town looking for a woman, or angry know-it-alls on the phone who love to call and shout at you. That's what my colleagues have seen and heard regarding this nation, and they've based their opinion on that. I met this kind of bias towards the UK many times during my travels; people see them as being loud, rowdy, impolite drinkers during their holidays, and arrogant bosses who think they are better than others in their own country. I saw and heard it every single time I left London for a holiday, and I still see it to this day.

I, on the other hand, leave it be. I've met too many wonderful English people in order to even compare them to the ones that, unfortunately, show up elsewhere.

Just as I did eight years ago in London, I've had to start from scratch. I don't have to squat here in Estonia – I have money to rent my own small place – but when it comes to work and its people, I've had to give up on a lot of customs that I learned in London, because they are too weird here. For example, hugging. Fucking hell. I remember when I first went to London, I didn't understand why you needed to greet someone with a hug when you'd already said hello. Now, I can't imagine any other way. My body spreads out its arms and wants to lock them with somebody as soon as I hear the words 'Hi' or 'Hello'. It's only when I'm halfway through the weird, one-sided hug that I understand how bizarre and emotionally desperate I must look amongst these discreet Estonians.

Once again, I've had to restart and reteach my brain on what 'normal' is and what is expected of me socially. And even though you'd say it's just going back to the style you came from, well... you'll never watch space in the same way once you've been to the Moon, I guess. Something inside of you has drifted, changed, and can't ever go back fully to what it was before.

Of course, with the growing popularity of my country amongst foreigners, the right-wing politicians have started to gain power as well. 'They have come here to take our jobs,' is like an international slogan that every country loves to babble about the incoming immigrants. 'They are a nuisance and they will never fit in,' is another. From the moment I returned to Estonia, all I heard was how eastern Europeans take UK jobs, Ukrainians take Estonian jobs, Estonians take Finnish jobs, everybody takes everybody's jobs...

I see my co-workers, who have come here to supposedly 'take my job', having to listen to the shit thrown at them in the media and, sometimes, in public, too. Now, I am in the position where I can see the same scenario as it was in London, only from another angle.

And guess what? It's all one big load of bollocks. I have been on both sides of this shit sandwich and it's all a frigging joke. Nobody came to this country to take my job. All I had to do was apply, show up for the interview, and not screw it up completely. I didn't have to fight for it with anybody. I was good enough myself to take it and get it. And yet people who haven't even applied for the job, whine and hate the ones that did.

All I can say to those haters is one thing: shut up and take the job yourself, if you want it so much. Believe me when I say this (and I really do know what I'm talking about in this case): leaving your life as it is behind, with all the people, places, and traditions you might have had, to go live in a completely new place that you know nothing about, is hard. *HARD*. You have no safety net like the locals do. As a matter of fact, all the odds are against you. In addition to being stressed out at work, you are also stressed out at home, because it never feels like a home. You still might not have friends or people to lean on. You feel like a floating existence without a safe place, yet you need to function as well, if not even better, than the others who have everything you are missing out on. Locals, who already knows the system and the people, are far ahead of these others. Just apply. And show up for the interview. Sometimes, that is all the local needs to do – but many of them find even that too much to ask.

When it comes to me taking the precious English jobs (of which I had many), I got them only because nobody else took them. I was never so good at any of my jobs that I wouldn't have been fired if they had found somebody else. But they didn't. Every single place I worked at was short-staffed. We constantly had a note on our bakery's window looking for more workers, yet nobody really wanted the job. It was so normal for people to not even show up to their trial shifts or interviews, that we weren't even surprised. And the fact was that if they had an English accent, we were about 80% sure they weren't gonna come – and they didn't. It's no wonder we only had four English girls out of the nine working there.

Do you want to work for an agency? Go to gigs, historical places? Do you want to see how the top 1% live and party? Be my guest. Agencies are constantly looking for people to work for them. Go ahead, take the job. It's already yours, if you can handle wearing that horrible minion costume.

It was the same situation with the pub. We were always in need of more help, yet people didn't show up on numerous occasions, nor did they ever say why. So every single one of us often did the work of three people.

Every place I worked at had its books open at all times for everybody to join. As we were constantly struggling at the bakery and the pub, and saw the recruitment very closely, I came to understand that Sean's words about the English being very picky and not wanting to do many jobs, was *very* accurate. It's true. Because I saw so many times myself how the people with English accents promised, yet never delivered, whereas the immigrants promised little, yet always delivered. And so the foreigners got the job, just simply because they showed up and gave it a try.

So, to be told 'You came here to take my job' is a sentence that will never hold any truth for me whatsoever.

And to all the haters out there who disagree with me, if you don't like what you see, change it then. Do that job yourself. Take it 'back' from them. Why didn't you take your job from me while you had the chance? Do it.

Not interested?

Didn't think so.

Don't get me wrong, I think patriotism is good. As a citizen of a country that has been invaded and ruled by many outer forces, I am very proud to call myself Estonian and appreciate its true culture, language, and ethnicity. I love telling foreigners about our struggles and survival, and I always will. I think every country should be proud of its heritage. That is what makes this world unique and interesting. It is the reason why we travel, so we can experience something new. My motto is, when in Rome – act as the Romans do. This applies to when I am travelling or living in another country.

But patriotism goes wrong if it turns into nationalism and racism. If one starts idolising one colour or nationality above the other, and starts putting others down. This is where it all goes to shit. This is the game politicians love to play, so they can create a problem and make themselves look like the good, productive guys, instead of focusing on the real issues.

I don't have faith in politicians – not in the UK, Estonia, US, or any other country, for that matter. I don't believe in the left or the right wing, the Tories or the Labourites. For me, life isn't that black and white. As they say, 'God's zoo is very colourful.' It is people that like to label everything, including each other, and put everything in boxes. And it is the politicians who play power games on these assumptions, creating enemies out of each other just so they can look good and be in power.

I have no desire to be anybody's muppet. If there is anything I learned from my one month on the journalism course in the university, it is to keep your eyes open at all times, to every situation, to everybody. We all have a story. We are all good people. And don't fully believe everything you read… no matter the source.

There are things I agree with both on the left as well as the right side. Nothing is as black and white as they try to make out. At the end of the day, we all want the same things for ourselves and our loved ones; it doesn't matter which side you are on.

Neither side wants to start a war, actually. Neither side wants to destroy the world. Our whole lives are blended between those two sides, covered in many colours – always has been and always will. So why don't we just accept it and move on? Leave the politicians to deal with the actual problems that need to be sorted out in every country – health services, education, employment, homelessness. These are the issues that can hit us all at any time, no matter our colour or nationality.

I remember a story I heard at the comedy bar once. I had been back in Estonia for a few months and didn't feel too good about the political situation in either the UK or Europe in general. All of a sudden, this Australian comedian told us his racist, yet ridiculous story of how he became friends with a guy who was all dressed up in Nazi clothes and memorabilia. All it took was to compliment his jeans and say one word in Estonian for this Nazi-dressed boy to soften up to the comedian, a guy from a completely different place than him, a guy he, supposedly, should have hated instead.

It was funny. It reminded me of my own moments when people would treat me in a certain way until I got to speak to them. Whether it was for work or for fun. Assumptions are absolutely nothing.

I always considered myself privileged – I'm white, from Europe, I didn't have to fight to get a good education; I've always had a warm bed to sleep on, and food to eat. The most I had to worry about was petty things, such as how to get my crush's attention or how to get through school without failing. All it took for me to burst that little safe bubble was to leave my safe zone and adventure outside. Then I understood the multiple layers of bigotry, and what politics is about.

We are all minorities in something, whether that is our appearance, accent, opinion, whom we love, or what we do. There are billions of people in this world, all with their imperfections and quirks; it would be impossible for everybody to be the same! And why should we be? We are not robots. This world is much better with all the weirdness that comes with uniqueness. Perhaps once the digital world creates robots to take over the world, there will be a place that is run in a certain way – the perfect way. But I doubt that even then everything would work.

Until then, we should all take a step back, and accept and enjoy all our quirks and differences. At the end of the day, you attract more bees with honey than you do with vinegar - whatever the attraction is that you're selling.

And, oh, if you wonder what happened to my French dream – who knows? I am a young woman living in Europe. I can go wherever I wish, as long as I have few euros in my back pocket. I am a citizen of the world. It's good to be in the European Union.

Acknowledgements

~

I would like to thank everybody who helped me make this book happen. Most of all, it's my auntie who kept me motivated all the way - you were one of the only ones I dared to show my writing to and who gave me good feedback regarding it.

Thanks to the comedian Louis Zezeran for letting me use his story about his new Nazi friend. Coming to the Comedy Estonia shows was what kept me going when I felt like an absolute shit myself, so you guys helped me in many ways.

But most of all, I want to thank my people at the Railway - you know who you are. These few chapters will never describe how crazy our days at the pub were, but may they be a little homage to our time spent there. You guys mean a lot to me and are the reason why there was a story to tell in the first place. Your love and the hate from the Brexiteers is the reason why this book exists at all! I guess time will show whether this was good or not...

All the people mentioned in the book either by their name or anybody who recognizes themselves in the story, I thank you all for being part of my journey. It's been one helluva ride. And I'm sure there will be more.

9 781839 752247